Josephine Whitely-Fields, PhD, MDiv

PIONEER BLACK CLERGYWOMEN

Stories of Black Clergywomen of the
United Methodist Church 1974 - 2016

WESTBOW
PRESS®
A DIVISION OF THOMAS NELSON
& ZONDERVAN

WestBow Press books may be ordered through booksellers or by contacting:

WestBow Press
A Division of Thomas Nelson & Zondervan
1663 Liberty Drive
Bloomington, IN 47403
www.westbowpress.com
844-714-3454

Scripture quotations taken from The Holy Bible, New International Version® NIV® Copyright © 1973 1978 1984 2011 by Biblica, Inc. TM. Used by permission. All rights reserved worldwide.

ISBN: 978-1-6642-1908-3 (sc)
ISBN: 978-1-6642-1909-0 (hc)
ISBN: 978-1-6642-1907-6 (e)

Library of Congress Control Number: 2021900411

Print information available on the last page.

WestBow Press rev. date: 01/22/2020

CONTENTS

CONTENTS

DEDICATION

To book is dedicated to the memories of my late parents, **Arthur Thomas Whitely, Sr.** and **Luella Braggs Whitely**, whose tender love and care was the foundation of my spiritual formation and provided the fundamentals of my lifelong quest for an ever-deepening relationship with God the Father, Son, and Holy Spirit.

And to my late husband, **Rev. Frederick Lee Fields**, whose awesome love and support undergirded me and my ministries, and we were blessed to build the kingdom of God together.

ACKNOWLEDGMENTS

The idea for this book resulted from an awareness of the void of autobiographical and biographical information regarding Black clergywomen. Stories in this book have been collected of Black clergywomen in the United Methodist Church since the 1968 dissolution of the Central Jurisdiction within the merged Methodist Episcopal and United Brethren Churches now known as the United Methodist Church.

My sincere thanks and appreciation to the clergywomen who graciously shared their stories resulting in this written historical legacy of Black clergywomen. Their short stories are vivid depictions of pioneer leaders.

The volunteer participants were invited to tell their life stories, in two phases, utilizing questionnaires. Phase 1 covers date of birth until answering the call to ordained ministry. Phase 2 covers answering the call to ordained ministry from 1974 until 2016. Their stories are recorded in response to those questions and according to their ordination dates for comparative and chronological analysis. The stories of volunteers who participated in both phases are included in this book. Other volunteer stories of those who participated in only one of the phases are housed in the archives of the General Commission of Archives and History and the General Board of Higher Education and Ministry.

Acknowledgment is given to the General Board of Higher Education and Ministry, and to the General Commission of Archives and History of the United Methodist Church who partially funded this historical project.

All proceeds benefit Black clergywomen scholarships.

ENDORSEMENTS

Dr. Josephine Whitely-Fields is a long-time influential leader in the United Methodist Church and in theological education. She has simultaneously lived the unique experience of Black clergywomen and worked to shape the field for those who have followed. This book gives voice to several Black clergywomen who have served our denomination and have faithfully summoned it to more fully live into its ideals and commitments.

Dr. Whitely-Fields recognizing the different phases of pastoral call and practice, identifies the unique challenges Black women face in local church ministry. While not shying away from enduring matters of systemic racism in the denomination, this book reflects the joy to be found in ministry for those who work tirelessly to help us to become the Church God calls us to be.

JAY RUNDELL, PRESIDENT
METHODIST THEOLOGICAL SCHOOL IN OHIO

We all have a story. But some stories drown out the stories of other. This volume narrates the stories of nine Black clergywomen, including four bishops, and elevates not only their stories but helps us to listen attentively for and to the stories we have not yet heard from women. Let those with ears hear and grow rich in appreciation and admiration.

BISHOP GREGORY PALMER, WEST OHIO EPISCOPAL AREA

This book is a treasure chest. To read these true accounts, compiled by Rev. Dr. Josephine Whitely-Fields, is to accept precious gifts of trust, friendship, vulnerability, and love that will serve to strengthen your life and your faith. I commend to you the accounts of these godly women for you to honor, respect, and listen well to the wisdom in their voices, knowing that for every account listed here, there are other voices not yet heard.

REV. PAT NELSON, GREENSBURG DISTRICT SUPERINTENDENT,
WESTERN PA CONFERENCE

Dr. Josephine Whitely-Fields ushers us into the reality of the making of Black women in ministry. Her writing style is pedagogical in nature and quickly captivates us as the challenging journey of the Black clergywomen is well documented and accurately researched.

Readers are afforded the opportunity to take an in-depth look into the personal lives of these clergy women through this anthological style must read. This book is multidimensional in scope examining the lives of these women from birth to adulthood. Personal stepping-stones into the ministry journey are provided to the audience, as we saunter through the corridors of challenging experiences.

As these Black clergy women give access into their personal lives and share their personal struggles against all the isms(racism, sexism, ageism, classism, and economic discrimination,) Dr. Josephine conversely invites us to experience their breakthroughs, victories, and blessings. Though they have endured hardship, their love for God, His people, and his church remained in the forefront, as they walked out their call.

DR. BEV DUFFEY-MARTIN, AUTHOR, SENIOR PASTOR,
MARANATHA WORSHIP CENTRE, DAYTON, OH

Again, America's institutional foundations are experiencing a reckoning for its systemic racism. This book encourages Black clergywomen to "keep their dignity in a dominant White environment." Rev. Dr. Josephine Whitely-Fields has written this book as a reference tool for those who have direct power and influence over the placement, entrance, and appointments of Black clergywomen. Simultaneously, Black clergywomen can use this book as a tool for self-examination and guidance.

DR. ANGEL DELACRUZ, PASTOR,
ELDERTON PRESBYTERIAN CHURCH, ELDERTON, PA

In these pages you will meet courageous Black clergywomen who responded to God's personal call to ministry by leaning on the Holy Spirit to overcome prejudices and to serve Jesus faithfully and powerfully.

RICHARD THOMAS, COORDINATOR,
WESTERN PA RENEWAL FELLOWSHIP

INTRODUCTION

Black clergywomen are pioneers of the United Methodist Church who continue to significantly contribute to making disciples and spreading the good news of the Gospel of Jesus Christ. Their stories are inspiring illustrations of the Holy Spirit at work in ordinary people who said yes to ordained ministry, beginning as pastors. It can be consistently observed that Black clergywomen are also prayer warriors engaging in extended periods of prayer and fasting.

Black clergywomen have positively impacted churches and communities while spiritual, numerical, and financial growth—in Black and White churches—occurred under their leadership. These victories and accomplishment were made possible by the intervening power of God, through their prayers, hard work, and perseverance along with the efforts of other women and men of various races and cultures in the United Methodist Church, other faith persuasions, and members of the greater society.

Black clergywomen are everyday soldiers on the front lines fighting to dismantle racism, sexism, ageism, and economic discrimination in a predominately White male vocation. They have experienced verbal abuse, false accusations, physical attacks, sexual harassment, marginalizing when racism occurs, and other acts of injustice. Their continuance demonstrates their strong commitment to the call to follow Jesus and love all of God's people.

The voices of Black clergywomen need to be heard, and their stories need to be preserved to provide a written legacy for present and future generations. These autobiographies and biographies are snapshots of the ordination processes and ministries from 1974–2016.

Black clergywomen's life stories are valuable resources. Their stories can give knowledge and understanding to judicatory authorities, seminary administrators, general church leaders, and church members for concretely addressing racism, sexism, ageism, economic discrimination, and other "isms" that Black clergywomen experience, and to help facilitate the church in moving forward together.

The life stories can be inspirational for present and future Black clergywomen, and other clergywomen of color, and fortify them for the battle of equality, equity, and justice in the church. Also, the stories can be utilized as a text for women's studies, church history, African American studies, and other classes in seminaries and universities.

In addition, these life stories can be helpful for any person, male or female, contemplating ordained ministry. Further, these stories give insights into some common faith principles of Christian people regardless of race, gender, age, or socioeconomic status. These stories can encourage any Christian to continue to work toward dismantling racism, sexism, ageism, and economic discrimination within the church as we continue building the beloved community. Activists for social justice can be strengthened as they see that the fight for justice and equal rights has been occurring in United Methodist churches across America.

Finally, recording these Black clergywomen's stories provides a way to hear their voices, preserves a section of history that otherwise could be lost, and establishes a written legacy of history in progress.

The United Methodist Church was formed in 1968 with the union of the Methodist Episcopal Church and the Evangelical United Brethren Church. However, since that time, ordination of Black clergywomen has been slow, and even in 2020, Black clergywomen are still making history in all levels of church and seminary life. In a study conducted by the General Commission on Religion and Race in 2011, their latest released study, it indicates there were only 2.3 percent Black clergywomen in the United Methodist Church. The General Board of Higher Education and Ministry, in 2017, stated there were only approximately seven hundred Black clergywomen in the United Methodist Church.

Black clergywomen serve as bishops, district superintendents, pastors, conference and general board staff, seminary professors and administrators, and in other official capacities. Some serve as role models and are heralded as pioneers and prayer warriors in those respective duties. We respectfully honor and acknowledge those who have been elected as bishops and appointed as district superintendents. Those serving as pastors of local churches do not get the same notoriety as those in high-profile positions, but their contributions are equally as important as they serve the grass roots of our faith, beginning with our children and youth, and serve faithfully until the members transition to glory.

All have and are paving the way as pioneers. Black clergywomen are inherently unsung heroes of the faith.

Clergywomen were invited to tell their stories, on a volunteer basis, who attended national meetings in 2017: Black Clergy Women of the United Methodist Church; Black Methodists for Church Renewal; and/or Sacred Sisters.

The stories involved personal interviews covering two phases. Phase 1 covers their lives from birth until the acceptance of the call to ordained ministry. Phase 2 covers the time after accepting the call until 2016. Both phases utilize personal interviews with a questionnaire format. The clergywomen are featured in chronological order of ordination, and their stories include the questions to facilitate comparative analysis.

I conducted the interviews as author of the book. I accepted the call, in 2016, to collect these stories as my labor of love in establishing a written legacy of Black clergywomen in the United Methodist Church of the United States of America.

I retired, in 2015, after forty years of ministry as a United Methodist ordained elder, having pastored churches in three states, ministered as director of missions and outreach of The Western Pennsylvania Annual Conference, served as founder/CEO of four 501(c)(3) nonprofit corporations within the Western Pennsylvania

Annual Conference, and was associate dean of doctoral studies, and adjunct faculty at United Theological Seminary in Dayton, Ohio. I hold a PhD in formative spirituality; Master of Divinity; Master of Arts in religion; Master of Arts in formative spirituality, and an equivalent Doctor of Dental Medicine.

Since the global protests for justice, following the death of George Floyd, the United Methodist Church has intensified its commitment to dismantle racism, but the question still remains: "How will the specific dismantling of racism, sexism, ageism, and economic discrimination, against Black clergywomen, be addressed?"

PHASE 1

Life stories beginning at birth and covering the years until the clergywomen accepted the call to ordained ministry:

> Then I heard the voice of the Lord saying, "Whom shall I send? And who will go for us?" And I said, "Here am I. Send me!" (Isaiah 6:8)

PHASE 2

Covers the life stories of Black clergywomen from the time they accepted the call to ordained ministry until 2016:

> The Spirit of the Lord is on me, because he has anointed me to preach good news to the poor. He has sent me to proclaim freedom for the prisoners and recovery of sight for the blind, to release the oppressed, to proclaim the year of the Lord's favor. (Luke 4:18–19)

CHAPTER ONE

Bishop Linda Lee

Retired Bishop
Years of Service at Retirement: 39+
Age: 68
Year accepted the call to ordained
ministry: 1980; Year ordained: 1986

PHASE 1

1. Recall significant events in your life and society, by decades, beginning with years 1–10, 10–20, and so on, until the year you accepted the call to ordained ministry, even if your earlier years were not in a Christian setting. List any songs that were formative in the life events you include in your stories.

YEARS 1–10

From age one to ten, living in West Philly, church and school were very important in my life. Singing in the church choir, taking violin lessons, playing in the orchestra at school, and recitals were also important and fulfilling for me during those years. I remember my relationships with the children and the people at my church as life-giving and joy-filled for me.

I have one brother, and we hung out together. We got along very well and were very compatible. We rarely had any kind of disagreements. We just hung out, playing games or cards. And we loved watching TV.

My mother was the church person. She was the one who made sure that we had a church home and that we got to church. She went to church also, but we usually didn't get to Sunday school. I was in the choir and in the youth group. The first pastor in my childhood retired shortly after we began to attend the church. However, he influenced me in terms of gaining a positive racial identity as a child in the fifties. He went to Africa and brought back slides of what Africans actually looked like and what the country [he visited] looked like. Instead of telling us, he brought the children to the front to look at the slides. Consequently, I developed a different view of Africa than what was depicted in *Tarzan* movies and other negative images of Black people popular at the time. I felt good about being a person of African descent.

The next pastor allowed me to teach vacation Bible school (VBS) when I was nine or ten years old to the youngest class at VBS that summer. Apparently, he recognized something in me that made him feel it was okay to do so. I don't know what he saw, but he allowed me to teach—with adult supervision, of course. I never forgot him for allowing me to do that, which was very helpful to my self-esteem at the time. His faith in me made me feel a part of the congregational community and that I was loved and included. I wanted to be active because I felt I had something to offer that was valued by the pastor and the congregation.

My father refused to go to church because of his experiences with the pastors he encountered in his hometown when he was growing up. He didn't trust them and didn't like them, so he never went to church with us. For him, going to church was not a part of his way of life.

YEARS 10–20

Ages ten to twenty were during the civil rights era, and I was still active in church. Music was still a part of my life, including playing the violin. The civil rights movement had begun, so things on television about the people in the marches being fire-hosed, attacked with dogs, and other atrocities ignited my sense of righteous indignation and affected my sense of well-being. I woke up to the realities of injustice and a new understanding of what it means to be Black in the United States.

Riots happened in Cleveland during those years. A major one occurred right around the corner from my house. We could hear the gunshots from inside our house. After the riots ended, soldiers with tanks and weapons were stationed along our route to high school. As a teenager, my mother didn't allow me to get involved in marches and protests. Later on, especially after I answered the call to ministry, I got involved in groups to improve relationships between the races and to increase human rights for Black and other marginalized people. I believe the seeds for the passion that undergirded the recurring themes of equality and justice in my ministry started with those civil rights news reports and exposure to the Cleveland riots when I was a teenager.

YEARS 20–30

Between ages twenty-one and thirty, I got married, had my first child—a son—moved from Ohio to Pennsylvania, had another son and a daughter, and enrolled in the University of Pittsburgh. My spouse was in a PhD program, so while he was working on his degree, I studied music for two years. He and I graduated on the same day. He received a PhD, and I received a BA. My church attendance was low during those years, but it was during the years that my sons were toddlers, before my daughter was born, that I started looking for a church home again. I wanted my children to experience the same kind of supportive, loving community that I had experienced at church.

YEARS 30–40

In my early thirties, we moved to Dayton, Ohio. We joined a wonderful, spirit-filled, family-nurturing Black church that happened to be United Methodist. The church was Dixon United Methodist Church, and that was the church in which I received and answered my call to ministry, enrolled in United Seminary, and from which I was appointed to my first church, Residence Park United Methodist Church.

List any songs that were formative in the life events you include in your stories.

Songs played a significant role in my life. I remember singing "Stand Up, Stand Up for Jesus," as a child. I remember "In the Garden," which was my mother's favorite song, so I liked that one also. A few other songs that we used to sing at family reunions were memorable: "Lord, I Want to Be a Christian," "Pass Me Not, O Gentle Savior," and "Kumbaya." However, I think the ones that stand out more in my life are "My Hope Is Built on Nothing Less" and "It Is Well with My Soul." These are some of the ones that I tend to go back to over and over again.

2. Recall the people who significantly contributed to your Christian formation up to the acceptance of the call. Tell the stories of how they influenced your life.

My mother was the first one to contribute to my Christian formation. She was the person who made sure I knew about church and prayer. Mother believed in reading the scriptures and doing what it teaches about life as a Christian. I grew up understanding that is what I was supposed to do. She taught me to pray, and she taught me that God answers prayers. She also believed in God speaking to us through our dreams, and she would talk to me about her dreams. I would talk to her about my dreams, and in those conversations, I learned that dreams were ways that God speaks to me. Mother was my spiritual foundation who contributed significantly to the development of my faith.

Over time, Gandhi was a remote mentor. I read his biography in high school and was greatly influenced by his life. Martin Luther King Jr. was a remote mentor for me also. Later, when I read Martin Luther King Jr.'s biography, I learned that Gandhi was one of his mentors. Both men greatly influenced my pursuit and passion for advocacy of civil rights and dismantling racism.

There was a Black music teacher in elementary school. She was a beautiful, shapely, shining Black woman who wore big earrings. She said positive, affirming things to me in class or when she passed me in the hallway. I don't remember her name, but she was a very positive influence.

In high school, there was a journalism teacher who was a positive influence. He encouraged me to work in the bookstore and write articles for the high school newspaper. I also wrote an advice column and was one of the editors of our school newspaper. My journalism teacher influenced me in all those endeavors.

3. *Recall the people/events that significantly served to deter your affirming the call to ordained ministry.*

There were deterrents to my answering the call. The church culture, at the time I received my call, had just begun to ordain women as clergy. Also, I grew up in a family that was very patriarchal. My family did not affirm women doing things that men did, like being pastors. Also, my first husband had concerns.

Traditions of the church, family, society, and culture all contributed to deterring my affirming the call to ordained ministry.

4. *When you received the call to ordained ministry, did you respond yes immediately and take appropriate action? Why or why not?*

Did I respond immediately to the call? Well, no! I ran, like many people do, for a while. Partly because I didn't have an understanding of how to do what I was being called and inspired to do. Furthermore, family and culture told me that women didn't do stuff like that. So, I interpreted my call as a call to be a nun or to join the Peace Corps or something else other than ordained ministry.

Finally, in my late twenties and early thirties, I was looking for what to do with the rest of my life when I read Gandhi's biography. I also read Martin Luther King Jr.'s biography and *What Color Is Your Parachute?* I read all three books the same summer, trying to discern what my next steps were going to be.

After I finished Martin Luther King Jr.'s biography, I felt like the Holy Spirit asked me, "So what are you doing with your life?" And I answered, "Well ... not much." As a result of discernment and prayer regarding that, I understood that I was to go to seminary. It was after I had been in seminary for a semester that I got my call to ministry and understood it was a call to serve God as pastor of a congregation. I continued praying and said, "Okay, Lord, I understand you are calling me to be a pastor, and you know what I need."

I started seminary with no money and no way to pay for it. Shortly thereafter, I went to a BMCR meeting, and when I came back, there was a check in my box at school to pay for the past and the upcoming tuition. Furthermore, I never paid a cent for tuition the whole time I was in seminary. When graduation came, I had just enough money to buy a suit. In reflection, I know that was nothing but God answering my prayer.

5. *What was your occupation when you received the call, and what effect did it have on your response?*

I was in between things; I did not have a specific occupation. I worked in the community and in community centers that provided programs for youth. I was doing that type of community work, but I wasn't in a profession at the time.

6. *If you did not take immediate action to the call, recall the thinking/ rationale that caused resistance to your immediate response.*

As I stated in question 5, there were traditions of the church, family, society, and culture that did not affirm women in ministry as pastors.

I guess the other part was "my sin was ever before me," like Paul talked about. Not only were there numerous traditions of resistance, but I knew that I was not worthy of serving, like so many of us think at the time. I had to move through that inner resistance and reluctance and accept that God had called me anyhow. It was like God called Moses, who certainly was no saint, and called other people, all of whom, including myself, were and are sinners.

Between the scriptures, my inner wrestling with God, and some of the other people I got to know who were pastors, I came to realize, "Yes, even me!"

7. What occurred that enabled you to overcome the resistance to answering the call?

I was able to overcome my own resistance by receiving affirmation from people whom I talked with about the call. I also experienced God's love as he made it clear to me that this is what He wanted me to do. I had to forgive myself for the past and look to the future. God gave me some metaphysical signs that also affirmed his presence with me, such as broken lights that started to miraculously work that were not working before. There were other signs to let me know that God was speaking to me.

8. What was the time frame between receiving the call and saying yes with appropriate action?

It was probably fifteen years. I believe I actually received my call when I was in high school and reading Gandhi's and Martin Luther King Jr.'s biographies. I thought what I was sensing and feeling was calling me to the Peace Corps or to be a nun. That is when I actually got my call; but I had no framework for it, and I didn't understand. It took time, experiences, conversations, and all the other things I have already mentioned until I eventually, by the time I was approximately thirty, understood what the call was and took appropriate action.

9. What role did the church play in your answering or not answering the call immediately?

The church I was attending at the time when I answered the call was Dixon UMC in Dayton, Ohio. The pastor there actually may have seen the call because he kept giving me more responsibilities in the church—from children's choir to teaching vacation Bible school and then teaching Sunday school. When I told him that I felt like I was called, he was very affirming—and so was the staff-pastor-relations committee (SPRC). I would say the church was a very affirming environment my entire life. Whenever I was in church, it was always a place where I could share whatever gifts God had given me to share. When I expressed that I sensed that God was calling me to something, the people in the church responded positively.

10. Were there any spiritual disciplines that played a role in your resistance or acceptance of the call? Tell the stories.

The primary spiritual discipline for me was prayer, and prayer is what I did even when I didn't feel worthy. Prayer is what I did when I answered the call because I knew I couldn't do it without God— not without God, period. I believe my learning and practicing the spiritual disciplines of forgiveness, fasting, and prayer were very helpful in preparing for ministry. Other preparations included studying the Bible and times of silence. I did appreciate times of silence and being alone with God before it became a regular discipline in my life.

11. In retrospect, how do you see God's hand at work in your life that prepared you for ordained ministry?

I think a couple of things happened. Part of my story is that I was actually called before I was born—based on my mother's relationship with God. She had been barren for seven years and was praying to have a child. She went to a revival, and the minister at the revival told people that whoever came forward in prayer that night, whatever they prayed for, God would give it to them.

My mother went forward and asked for prayer to have a child, and the ministers prayed for her. Within a year, I was born, and like Hannah in the Old Testament, out of gratitude after I was born, my mother gave me back to God. After I had been elected a bishop, my mother asked me if I thought that her giving me back to God right after I was born (like Hannah had done with Samuel) had anything to do with the fact that I had been elected. I said, "Yes, I think it had everything to do with it." I still think so!

So, I think the call happened before I was even born and was played out over time in different ways and in different settings to get to the end that God had in mind—even up to and including being elected bishop.

The other part of the preparation was the different ways that I was able to relate to people growing up. I began giving people advice in elementary school about relationships and other things. Not that giving advice was necessarily preparation for ministry, but it gave me experience in relating to people. Of course, people do come to pastors for counsel; I noticed over my lifetime that people tended to come to me for counsel, and later for prayer and counsel. I also found that the Lord answered prayers as I prayed and counseled others.

The mistakes I made in life also prepared me for ministry. Choices I made as a result of having grown up in an alcoholic home, lessons I wasn't taught at home, but learned in the school of "life," all prepared me for the work and service of ministry.

God revealed things to me in dreams and visions that helped prepare me for ministry. I also had opportunities to lead different groups as president of different organizations. Therefore, I gained experience in leading groups of people.

So, there were different levels of preparation over time through different life experiences that prepared me for ministry. Every experience, every mistake, and every success came to be a resource after I answered the call.

12. *When you accepted the call to ministry, what was the response from persons in your life?*

Some were surprised. I had one person who couldn't believe that I was called to ministry. He said, "I know you. I remember you. I don't know how." He was incredulous that I could be called. He didn't actually know anything in particular about me, but he was in disbelief.

There were other people who said to me, "I knew it was going to happen" or "No, I'm not surprised" just because of how they experienced me. It was a kind of mixed response, which was really interesting.

My husband, at the time, had concerns. I knew that God had called me, and I knew I couldn't not answer. I had to decide to let the chips fall where they were going to fall in that situation.

My mother was supportive of me, although I was raised in a patriarchal family and she was more patriarchal than my father. One uncle in the family rejected the idea of me being a pastor or preacher entirely. He didn't want to deal with it at all.

I had an aunt who was an evangelist. She took me under her wing at a family reunion, and I had her as a role model to look up to. She affirmed me and celebrated my call. After a while, the rest of the family accepted my call, but not at the beginning.

PHASE 2

1. *Tell the story of your first three years while meeting the requirements necessary for elder's or deacon's ordination or for local pastor's requirements. What were some of your struggles and victories as you pursued answering the call?*

- *Share your stories with the Board(s) of Ordained Ministry. In what ways were they helpful? Did you have any identifiable issues that you were told to improve upon?*

- *If you were assigned to a church(s) during those first three years, what relationships did you have with the parishioners and the community?*
- *When you attended seminary or licensing school, what were your experiences with faculty, staff, and peers? Include the specific years.*

When I was attending Dixon UMC, the pastor and his wife supported me and gave me guidance so that I could answer the call.

When I went before the Board of Ordained Ministry, I was told to first complete a class in clinical pastoral education and come back. I was also told to work on expressing myself more clearly. The second interview went fine. I was learning to speak up and speak out.

United Seminary was a joy. I have great memories of United Theological Seminary in Dayton, Ohio. The educational experience was wonderful. I was particularly grateful for the cross-denominational environment with multicultural people. The seminary was also intentional about emphasizing inclusive language. The staff and faculty were affirming and supportive.

I had a husband and three young children while attending seminary, so that was a challenge at times. For instance, during my last year, I would put the children to bed and take a short nap. Then, I would arise and write papers from two o'clock until five o'clock in the morning. I would be so tired. I prayed, and God helped me write those papers. Even under those trying circumstances I received mostly B grades

2. *Share your stories of each individual appointment since beginning the process for ordination until 2016. Include the following:*

- *What lessons did you learn from each appointment?*
- *What meaningful relationships were established? Include personal, professional, and church member relationships.*
- *What were your personal and church financial state?*

- *Relate any successes or challenges you faced in each appointment. Were there any personal events that affected your ministry (weddings, deaths, or illnesses?)*
- *What Methodist, national, or world events affected your appointments? Explain how.*
- *Have any of the meaningful relationships established with your parishioners been continued over the years?*

The churches and/or extension ministries I served, until 2016 were as follows:

- Residence Park UMC, Dayton, Ohio.
- Methodist Theological School in Ohio, Delaware, Ohio.
- Central UMC, Detroit, Michigan.
- Conant UMC, Detroit, Michigan.
- Detroit East District Superintendent, Michigan Annual Conference.
- Resident bishop of Detroit and West Michigan Conferences.
- Resident bishop of Wisconsin Annual Conference.
- Bishop in residence at Garrett Theological Seminary.

FIRST APPOINTMENT:
PASTOR, RESIDENCE PARK UMC, DAYTON, OHIO

When I was appointed to Residence Park UMC, it was quite an adjustment for the church since I was the first woman to be appointed there.

I attended a conference at ITC where a woman professor conducted one of the workshops, and she gave some insight on my situation. She explained that most women were insecure about having a woman pastor in such close situations with their husbands. She suggested I court the women of the church—not in a sexual way—but in a way that would build trust among the women. I took her advice and began to make special efforts in ministering to the women of the church.

By the grace of God, I was able to win their trust and confidence. By the time I left Residence Park UMC, most of the people were very saddened to see me go.

Under my leadership, we emphasized leadership training and activities that fostered appreciation of our African American heritage. Within three years, the church doubled in membership.

At Residence Park UMC, I got to know and love the people deeply. The congregation experienced many losses in their families, and they had many health issues. It was very meaningful to pastor them. I experienced joy pastoring the church, but I struggled to get people to rally around ministry and embrace the vision. When I left, people had begun to grasp the vision.

I had good relationships with other Black UM pastors—and pastors in other denominations in Dayton—who welcomed me as the "new kid on the block." They already had a fellowship that met monthly and shared their journeys. The pastor of McKinley UMC helped me with my first funeral. The pastor of my home church was particularly helpful. I was also involved in the community and with other churches. Community pastors were mostly older Black men, but there was one Black Apostolic clergywoman who was a great inspiration and support to me. There was a Black clergywoman on the conference staff who was a wonderful mentor. I enjoyed working with all of them.

Financially, the church could only afford a part-time salary, but they were able to move to a full-time salary during my tenure. The church grew from fifty or sixty members to ninety-seven members.

In my personal life, I was moving toward divorce. However, I became a better preacher while learning to nurture the souls of the parishioners. I also implemented my skills in group and relational dynamics that enabled me to pastor families that were feuding without my getting directly involved in their feuding.

I was able to build good relationships within the church. After I left to serve my next appointment, and subsequent ones, I was invited back to preach on several occasions. I was able to say thank you and show appreciation on those occasions to both Dixon and Residence Park UM Churches.

Second Appointment:
Methodist Theological School in Ohio (MTSO)

My next appointment was at Methodist Theological School in Ohio (MTSO) as the assistant to the dean for educational administration. My responsibilities were to create the administrative structure for the Drug and Alcohol Abuse Ministries program. This was the first program of its kind at a seminary that allowed students to earn a Master of Arts degree with this focus. The position was new, and I was the first person to fill it. Therefore, I was also the first Black clergywoman to fill that position. It was a three-year commitment. Several faculty and staff provided great counsel and support. Those relationships—along with my own skills and experiences—made my ministry there a joy.

In that position, I also counseled students and staff. I worked with Black students to revise the curriculum to make it more relevant for the Black students. The faculty was receptive to hearing African American concerns, and they responded appropriately. Also, I started a gospel choir with an ethos of praise and served as the director. A quartet was also started under my advisement. On a personal note, I was divorced while at MTSO, becoming a single parent with three children—two sons in high school and a daughter in middle school. My oldest son graduated from high school while I was there. We attended church in Columbus, and the pastor and his wife were a blessing to our family. At the end of the three years, I was asked to come to Detroit.

Third Appointment:
Central UMC, Detroit, Michigan

My third appointment was to serve as associate pastor at Central UM in Detroit with a White senior pastor. The congregation was multiracial and very involved in the community. The church was intentionally active in social justice and in women's rights ministries. Also, there were ministries to the hungry population and to the homeless.

By then, both my sons had graduated from high school and gone on to college. So, my daughter and I moved together to Detroit. She went to Martin Luther King High School and later graduated from Wayne State University.

In Detroit, I had the opportunity to work with interfaith and ecumenical groups, including one with Gandhi's grandson on a peace event. This was significant for me because Gandhi and Martin Luther King Jr. were remote mentors for me through their writings.

The relationship with most of the members was great! It was a great experience meeting the people and working with the ministries to the hungry and homeless and working as peace advocates and with other ministries of that congregation.

Central UMC is also where I was serving when I met the man who is now my husband, at a BMCR meeting. Our wedding was at Central UMC, officiated by my bishop in Michigan and by my former bishop in Ohio. My husband and I will celebrate our twenty-ninth wedding anniversary as of this writing.

FOURTH APPOINTMENT:
ASSOCIATE PASTOR, CONANT UMC, DETROIT MICHIGAN

I was appointed at Conant UMC from 1992 until 1995. The church had started as a merger of two stronger churches twenty years before. The people did not want to merge, and after twenty years, there were still strong memories of the two different churches. They somehow remained merged, but they still talked of past memories and still related to the "sacred cows" of the two previous churches. When the two choirs were asked to merge, they both stopped singing. Therefore, a new choir was born in conflict. I fasted forty days for the Holy Spirit to break up the conflict. God answered my prayers. Even a couple of women who had left came back. I learned a lot about group dynamics in that situation.

There were many good experiences. The people were so faithful. One Sunday after church, the youth director transformed the fellowship hall into an indoor playground. The space became a sacred, holy, and safe place for the children. All of them—from our eighteen-year-old drummer to the toddlers—were running around, jumping rope, and playing ball and hopscotch. They all abandoned themselves to just having fun. It was particularly important for them that Sunday because we had just discussed gun violence in their schools and neighborhoods in the youth service. That indoor playground was truly holy ground for them that day. I officiated a wedding for a couple who had been married in their youth but never had a wedding. They were now in their sixties, and I was able to renew their vows for them as their first and only wedding at our church.

We worked together in interfaith ministries in the area, which provided good cultural interactions.

Additionally, the church ministries afforded new opportunities that resulted in expansion of my administrative skills. I developed good relationships with the leadership team, youth worker, organist, administrative staff, and members of the congregation. Unfortunately, there were also a few members with whom the relationship was strained and never healed. All these experiences were part of my development as a pastor and a person. I also developed working relationships with UMC pastors and other clergy in town. I was requested to teach theology in the continuing education program at one of the largest Baptist churches in town and at the Ecumenical Theological Seminary in Detroit. My DS was always supportive, offering counsel and recommendations. His input made the challenges that did arise easier to resolve.

In my personal life, I found an African American holistic medical doctor who was also a Black woman. She, and later, another woman doctor, were very instrumental in assisting me to practice better health care. I started regular exercise to ward off arthritis from an earlier car accident. I began fasting weekly and during liturgical seasons. I engaged in fasts for three to twenty-one days—and once for forty days. These disciplines enabled me to grow personally and professionally. Whenever I felt spiritual warfare going on, I increased my fasting and sensed the presence of angels on guard—or I just waited and watched God bring about God's divine solution.

Finances of the church were pretty good, and they set a goal of moving toward paying 100 percent apportionments. The church was intentional and included the apportionment increases in the budget. We did reach that goal. There were a couple hundred members, and the church was faithful and self-sustaining.

My salary, by that time, was midrange, and I was able to contribute to our needs as a family and even to pay off a tax debt I owed from the past.

During my tenure, the membership increased, and people of other cultures began joining the church. The adult and youth ministries were going well, and there was a gay couple active in the ministries of the church, allowing the church to be more inclusive.

I developed a strong relationship with an older woman in church. She had a strong belief that she kept constantly before me as she said, "Everything will be all right when the time is ripe." Not when the time was *right*, as I was accustomed to thinking, but when the time was *ripe*. For some reason, remembering that always gave me hope. I also had a strong connection with a young mother and her autistic son. Her love, care, and diligence in seeing that his needs were met were incredible. The child and I developed a very strong bond with each other, and when I saw his mother recently, she said he was in college and living independently.

FIFTH APPOINTMENT:
DISTRICT SUPERINTENDENT, DETROIT EAST DISTRICT

I was appointed to serve as the Detroit East DS from 1995 until 2000. I had responsibility for more than fifty congregations. My role changed from being a pastor of one community of people to functioning as an evangelist where I had to preach and connect to people I might not see but once a year.

I learned that the Holy Spirit could be found in places I didn't expect and not to judge a book by its cover. I found the Holy Spirit at the largest church in the conference and in the smallest rural church in the district. I also studied and developed additional skills in administration; conflict management; the establishment and maintenance of endowments; creative ways to fund ministries; and deepening of my understanding that it was possible for churches to establish good relationships, within the church and in the community, regardless of the size, culture, or race.

I developed meaningful relationships with the lay and clergy leadership on the conference and district levels. I found most of the leadership to be open and genuine. There were good ministry opportunities shared with Black, White, Latina, Native American, and Korean leadership, and I experienced the Black and White clergywomen to be very gracious.

The district was fun as I got to know the extended members of the conference. However, there were times when mean-spirited forces were at work behind the scenes, so we had to intervene to protect some of the pastors in those situations as well as having to protect or facilitate healing in some congregations from inappropriate pastoral behavior.

The finances of the district were fine, and money was available for identified ministry needs. As a district, we particularly worked on empowerment of the laity and youth. There was also some work accomplished with women and with pastors of color.

My personal salary was the same as all other district superintendents in the Detroit Conference. The salary was a very nice raise from previous positions.

On a personal level, the DMin, which I began at United Theological Seminary, while I was pastoring at Conant UMC, was completed while I was a DS. As a district superintendent, I learned I had to speak up in cabinet in regard to the congregations I had responsibility for and on behalf of people of color. I was the voice of color in the midst of very assertive White clergymen and one White clergywoman. I learned that if I did not speak up about certain things, no one would. So, I found my voice there. We learned to work together well with our bishop, diverse as we were.

Some successes and challenges I experienced included getting pastors assigned to some churches where there was resistance. I asked one congregation who did not want a pastor because he was Black,

"What does his color have to do with whether or not he has the gifts and skills needed to serve as your pastor? I am Black—would you have me as your pastor?"

"Yes," they said, "but you are different."

Needless to say, after talking, prayer, and the faithfulness of that congregation to their faith in Jesus Christ, the pastor was appointed, and they grew to love one another deeply.

It was encouraging to see most of the congregations rise to the occasion to live out their faith. Some churches that worked through conflict became stronger. Some other churches were mean-spirited and harmful, requiring intervention. In addition, clergy misconduct charges were challenging. Those misconduct charges resulted in some pastors being put on leave and/or requesting them to give up their orders. These situations were extremely discouraging and disappointing. However, some who were placed on leave later came back healed and went on to become stronger pastors.

There were some meaningful relationships established with a couple of pastors. We would call and chat with each other occasionally. Also, there was one district superintendent and his wife with whom I developed a close relationship. They understood the importance of claiming and walking in their heritage, and they understood the importance of me claiming and walking in mine. The wife even gave me a beautiful needlework of people of diverse cultures as a gift when I left the conference. My colleagues on the cabinet were respectful and supportive, and I felt the same for them.

In the spring of 1999, a woman prophesied I would have the highest office in church. I didn't take it too seriously because another Black woman was being groomed to get elected. I was prepared to vote for her. However, she died unexpectedly. In the fall, my bishop told me it was possible I might be asked to consider putting my name in to be considered for bishop. The Black clergywomen of the UMC convinced me to enter the nomination process for bishop. One of the clergywomen also prophesied that three Black women would be elected as bishops in 2000. They laid hands on us at the Jurisdictional Conferences in 2000, and that is exactly what happened.

SIXTH ASSIGNMENT:
ELECTION AS BISHOP IN THE NORTH CENTRAL JURISDICTION
OF THE UMC, ASSIGNED TO THE DETROIT AND
WEST MICHIGAN CONFERENCES

I was elected as a bishop out of the West Michigan Conference in 2000 and assigned as the resident bishop of the Michigan area, which included Detroit and the West Michigan Conferences. I served the Michigan area from 2000 until 2004. For a bishop to be sent back to the same conference where she or he had previously served had not occurred for at least forty years and required a special action of the Jurisdictional Conference.

There were pros and cons in returning to the same area. Having served previously as their district superintendent, I knew many pastors more personally than would have occurred had I been assigned to another area. Some pastors expected special favors, while others never adjusted to having a Black woman as their "boss." This was a particular challenge for some of the cabinet members. Not only had I just been their colleague—I was Black, female, and had a way of communicating that was very different than my predecessors. For example, there was more of an oral style of communicating before I was assigned, but I preferred to communicate in writing. There were a few who had trouble adjusting, but most adjusted well.

I quickly learned that, as bishop, I needed healthy relationships in the office, with a clear understanding of roles, and I needed someone I could trust. I had a good relationship with the director of connectional ministry, who was intentional in addressing me as bishop when I became bishop. In my culture, titles are used and important. I had a coach who was helpful and supportive of me as I entered another learning curve as bishop. However, there was an undercurrent of doubt regarding the administrative abilities I needed as bishop. The bishop who invited me to the cabinet as DS was supportive and has continued to be supportive even unto this day. There were a couple of Black bishops in the Council of Bishops that I developed mutually supportive relationships with, and a few others in the general church became good friends.

Other lessons I learned involved another level of church administration, organizational work, and the importance of a good office administrator. I continued to experience the intense gratitude of most church people. I also experienced that many people can be set in their ways. Each church has its own culture and is unique. I found many churches that were more interested in caring for each other than the community. They had to be encouraged to make decisions to connect to people they didn't know.

As bishop, I became more acutely aware of systemic racism and inequity in salaries, particularly for people of color and women clergy. Placing pastors in churches with salary deficiencies was more prevalent for Blacks and people of color. White clergy had more options for upward mobility. Racism was systemic throughout the church. I witnessed from a different level, that the church was a reflection of the culture, whereas I believed that as the church of Jesus Christ, we are called to lead the culture in the ways of Christ. I also witnessed inequities regarding the general conferences.

One time, one of the long-time bishops made a remark implying that I was one of the prophets in the midst of the Council of Bishops. I believe he said this because I didn't know any better than to name the inconsistencies I was seeing. For example, I once expressed my belief that a criticism I heard made about some others in the church be applied to ourselves as the Council of Bishops and general agency leaders.

While I was serving in Detroit, I had worked with the General Commission on Religion and Race (GCORR), became the president of the board of directors, and served as interim executive director of GCORR for five months when the executive director took a leave. I have given presentations for conferences and jurisdictions addressing ways to eradicate racism, and I have been doing that for a while. I was also chair of the Racism Task Force in the Council of Bishops and did some work there to help the council deal with issues of racism in the council, and eventually a statement was written. Addressing racism and seeking ways to dismantle racism in the United Methodist Church became a theme throughout my ministry, and I continue to be asked to speak to it, even in retirement.

The vision for the general conference was vitality and growth for the churches of our denomination. I saw us attempting to move in the right direction with this vision. As bishops and general agency leaders of the church, we had a distinct role in keeping the vision alive in the face of approval or criticisms.

I spoke out at one meeting about the fact that we market ourselves as a church with "open hearts, open minds, and open doors," but we don't model what we say. We are not modeling the slogan as it applies to homosexuals, Native Americans, African Americans, and others. When I was chair of the Council Task Force on Racism, which existed to address these kinds of concerns, the council voted to publish a statement of the council's position on racism. This same task force approved my editing of a book for the UMC entitled, *A New Dawn in Beloved Community*. It focused on ways to create "beloved community" in contemporary times. Five years later, the Council of Bishops did write and publish a statement on racism. As God would have it, I ended up being the person who presented it to the council for its unanimous vote of approval. It was sent out to the churches before we left that meeting.

While serving as bishop of the Detroit Conference, our cabinet shared mission trips to Haiti and to New Orleans after Hurricane Katrina to help restore one of the houses and visit with some of the United Methodist people and congregations that had been affected by it. Those were very meaningful ministries for us and those we visited, according to the feedback we received.

While bishop of the Michigan Area Conferences, I strongly emphasized the importance of taking a Sabbath day for a holistic approach to health. All clergy were required to attend a retreat that emphasized the Sabbath. Now many pastors take a Sabbath—even though initially they came kicking and screaming.

When our country experienced 9/11, I was at a clergywomen meeting in Baltimore. I was bumped up to an earlier flight on a plane from Baltimore to Detroit the morning the plane crashed into the Twin Towers. As a result, I was able to return home that day. My husband, on the other hand, was in New York that day and was stranded. He was not able to get back to Detroit for a week. As we suffered together that national and international tragedy, I met with the cabinet and staff members to plan pastoral care for pastors and church members in the conference. There were many interfaith events in Detroit and elsewhere across the US during the next few weeks. There was a sense of human solidarity across faiths and belief systems. From great tragedy, hope between cultures and races was born. It was an intense and complex time.

A few weeks later, when I was in my prayer room, taking my Sabbath, God spoke to me regarding my uneasiness in flying. He revealed that just as He had protected me from getting stranded— that he had saved me and protected me in the past—I had no need to have anxiety in flying. God was in control. I was delivered and set free from flying anxiety.

Financially, I received the salary established for all bishops; there could be no discrimination in bishop's salaries or in the salaries established for district superintendents within a given conference. The bishop's salary was a significant raise from my salary as district superintendent.

In 2003, my mother passed in Cleveland. Prior to her death, her foot was amputated, then her leg just below the knee. I went to Cleveland once a week. The night that she died, she came to me in a dream—with both legs—and she was dancing. Shortly after Easter, we went to Cleveland where we had her funeral. I was deeply grateful to see that most of the bishops in my College of Bishops had come to share that time with me and my family, along with family and friends who brought their love and support.

I conducted my annual conference sessions for that year and then went on retreat for some time apart. This was a very traumatic time for me, but many people were supportive of me during my time of grief. It took at least a year to get over her death and come back somewhat to myself.

SEVENTH ASSIGNMENT:
RESIDENT BISHOP OF THE WISCONSIN CONFERENCE

I was assigned as resident bishop of the Wisconsin Conference from 2004–2012. For the most part, the Wisconsin Conference had little experience in relating to Black people. However, meaningful relationships were developed with cabinet members. Our conference sponsored a mission trip to India that was also a great cultural experience. A new communications director was assigned in the conference, and that person presented the conference and the ministries of the conference in a more positive way, which helped the conference to better appreciate its progress.

Lessons I continued to learn were the complexity of human relationship; how seriously people can hold on to convictions at the expense of others; and how people can positively and negatively adapt to unexpected changes.

During their annual meetings, relationships were established with pastors of color, women clergy, and the conference youth. My personal friends were mostly out of town because I was gone extensively.

I became aware of the fact that some people were of the mindset that being spiritual and Black could not be equated with good administration. Other people wanted to tell me how to administrate the conference—even though they had never been bishops themselves. There were others who wanted to change the church's stance on homosexuality. The UM church, in general, was going through times of conflict over that issue, and it continues today.

Some successes I experienced were some healing of relationships in the Wisconsin Council, which had become so divided over the homosexuality issue. I had to take action on same-sex marriage issues. The annual conference had a trial and developed a plan for a covenant relationship. I preached and emphasized that we should strive to be one despite differences. I encouraged the differing sides to talk to each other, which was a major accomplishment. I was also able to help facilitate an inexpensive trial. All these issues were highly publicized via various forms of public media and continue to be issues in the UMC in the United States of America.

As bishop, I would hear what the people had to say, but I would not take sides because I was bishop to all, regardless. Some people did not like me taking a neutral position.

I had decided after I was elected bishop that I would serve for twelve years and then retire. In 2012, I did not feel that I needed to retire, but I felt pressured to do so. Looking back, I know that God used that experience to get me where God wanted me to be. My decision to retire created the space for my next divine assignment.

EIGHTH AREA OF MINISTRY:
BISHOP IN RESIDENCE, GARRETT THEOLOGICAL SEMINARY

In 2012, after my retirement, I accepted a position at Garrett Theological Seminary as bishop in residence. During the fall of 2012 and the winter of 2013, I finished editing *A New Dawn in Beloved Community*. In addition, I completed the United Methodist two-year Spiritual Formation Academy before my position at Garrett began. My required project was to create a retreat model for clergywomen of African descent. That project became a ministry of the church in the Black experience at Garrett.

I began my tenure as bishop in residence at Garrett Evangelical Theological Seminary in the spring of 2013. My primary responsibility was to counsel students who were recommended to me by the president of the seminary, or by faculty, for spiritual counsel and guidance. Students could also receive counsel from me about general appointments or disciplinary questions related to their ordination or commissioning process. A couple of professors invited me to give guest lectures on the topics of Sabbath, self-care, and church polity. I also taught DMin intensives on the subject of spiritual formation and leadership. I was also invited to attend and offer input in faculty meetings and lead seasonal retreats for Lent and Advent seasons. My experiences at Garrett were very positive ones, and I had a meaningful connection to the president, faculty, students, and staff. My role was "chaplain" in that setting, and it seemed to be a good fit for all of us.

I experienced a personal health challenge, and I had to intentionally focus on being more active to counteract the excess amount of sitting. There were no challenges professionally. I did address racism with the seminary leadership, but there was already an openness and interest on the part of the president, and the faculty to deal with the inequities they were aware of.

Notable successes were giving leadership at a prayer vigil for the staff and faculty; the number of counselees (staff and faculty); and the number of students who sought me out to tell their stories. Some of the seminary relationships continue until today, including professors and students.

In 2014, the Sacred Sisters clergywomen ministry was born. Such a gathering had been on my heart for ten years before it came to fruition. This ministry began as an opportunity to reach clergywomen of African descent, in the North Central Jurisdiction, but quickly grew to be a national gathering. There are currently about eight peer support groups within the US, which developed as result of attendance at the annual Sacred Sisters retreat.

Some of the experiences Sacred Sisters offers at the annual retreat include:

- Getaway time from our congregations/extension ministries/other ministry settings and from every day cares and concerns.
- Compassionate and shared sacred conversations in a quiet space.
- Culturally relevant worship and learning sessions.
- Peer-support groups.
- Walks, restorative yoga, and other exercise opportunities.
- Pampering sessions.
- Rest and renewal.
- A year of mentoring, support. and resources designed to encourage wellness.

- Explore sacred rituals that will strengthen spiritual practices and collective advocacy for justice in ministry areas.

3. Do you see any of your life stories depicted in the lives of the saints in the Bible? Was it helpful to see yourself in scripture as you journeyed in your appointment?

When I was a district superintendent in Michigan, I prayed for the Lord to show me a metaphor for my ministry. I was given the story of the three Hebrew boys—Shadrach, Meshach, and Abednego—who were thrown into the fiery furnace but were not burned.

As bishop, I was given the metaphor of David and Goliath. I didn't slay the giant, but I was a prophetic voice to the giant. I offered what God wanted me to offer when in meetings, whether it was well received or not. I did get to see some of the prophetic things being addressed.

At Garrett, I did not receive a biblical metaphor, but I saw myself as the pastor and chaplain of the seminary community.

4. If you were the first Black woman, or among the firsts, in any of your appointments, state those firsts, and tell the stories. What words of wisdom would you pass on to others who may become pioneers during their ministry?

I was the first Black clergywoman in every ministry I served:

- First Black clergywoman pastor at Residence Park UMC in Dayton, Ohio.
- First Black clergywoman at MTSO, in Delaware, Ohio, as administrative assistant to the dean.
- First Black clergywoman as associate pastor at Conant UMC in Detroit, Michigan.
- First Black female DS in Detroit, Michigan.
- First Black clergywoman elected as bishop in the North Central Jurisdiction.

- First Black female bishop assigned to the Detroit and West Michigan Conferences.
- First Black female bishop assigned to the Wisconsin Area.
- First Black female bishop to serve as bishop in residence at Garrett Seminary.

What words of wisdom would you pass on to others who may become pioneers during their ministry?

- Be true to yourself. One area that I compromised after I was elected bishop was to discontinue wearing African apparel daily because I felt it was a distraction. I then only wore my garments on occasion—or when I was led to do so. If I had to do it over again, I would wear the African garb as I had been doing, including the day I was elected. I feel now that would have allowed me to continue to be even more fully my authentic self than I was while I served in that role.
- Help people to keep their dignity no matter who they are.
- Develop a good support system. Maintain close personal friends that you can pray with and with whom you can be accountable to one another.
- Continuously pursue training to equip yourself for the demands of your ministry setting(s).
- Remember that God is ultimately the One we must answer to.

5. *In hindsight, how could the annual conference and/or other UM personnel be more helpful when assigning Black clergywomen as firsts in a given area of ministry?*

- There should be discussions regarding culture and gender, before the assignment, with the clergywoman and the leadership of the church and/or extension ministry.
- There should be specific resources for the health and safety of the Black clergywoman in the community to which she is being appointed.

- The bishop and cabinet should be committed to being intentionally aware of the ministry context the Black clergywoman is appointed to in order to be appropriately supportive to the pastor and the congregation.
- If any conflict should arise, the bishop and cabinet will listen to and consider the perspective of the clergywoman before any action is taken.

6. *What personal gifts and graces have been assets to you during your years of ministry? Be specific and relate how they have been helpful.*

- I have a genuine interest in people.
- I am an administrator.
- I have the gift of mediation.
- I actively listen and strive to hear what is being said.
- I tend to see the big picture of what is happening now and how it applies to the future.
- I seek to help people to stretch themselves beyond their comfort zones in a gentle way.
- I have the ability to see and interpret how the dots connect.
- I have intuitive gifts that allow me to help others to see how to accomplish their goals.
- I am patient and encouraging with groups as they work at accomplishing their goals.
- Last, but not least, God is my source and my greatest resource.

7. *List any particular accomplishments or honors conferred during your years of ministry.*

- National BMCR: Distinguished service on board of directors.
- Black Clergywomen of the UMC Organization: Elected as the first chair of the current body.
- First Black clergywoman appointed as district superintendent of the Detroit East District.

- First Black clergywoman bishop elected in the North Central Jurisdiction of the UMC.
- First Black clergywoman to serve as bishop of the Detroit and West Michigan Conferences.
- Black clergywomen of the UMC Organization, served as bishop liaison.
- First Black clergywoman to serve as bishop in residence at Garrett Theological Seminary.
- Founder of Sacred Sisters: a ministry of and for clergywomen of African descent.

In addition, as bishop on the Wisconsin Council of Churches, I helped facilitate conversations for the AME Church to become a member of the council and celebrated when the AME Church became a member of the council.

CHAPTER TWO

Rev Dr. Josephine Ann Whitely-Fields

Retired Elder

Years of Ministry Prior to Retirement: 40

Conference: Western Pennsylvania Annual
Conference, Cranberry Township, Pennsylvania

Age: 73

Year accepted the call to ordained ministry: 1974

Year Ordained: 1986

PHASE 1

1. *Recall significant events in your life and society, by decades, beginning with year 1–10, 10–20, etc., until the year you accepted your call to ordained ministry, even if your earlier years were not in a Christian setting. List any songs that were formative in the life events you include in your stories.*

YEARS 1–10

I was born in 1944, the fifth of nine children, in Caretta, West Virginia, a small, rural coal-mining area. My parents were loving and practicing Christians, and our family was raised the same way. We were a close-knit family, and we loved each other dearly.

Daddy worked in a neighboring town, and he left before the children got out of bed and barely returned before nighttime. Mother was a stay-at-home mom who also managed the finances. She taught us Christian values, prepared us to enter school, assisted with our homework, taught us how to cook and keep house, and taught us our Sunday school lessons. I remember her instilling in us that we could be anything we wanted to be with God's help. Mother also taught us that whatever we chose to be in life would be fine with her just as long as we were the best we could be. In fact, she taught us two life mottoes:

- I can do everything through him who gives me strength (Philippians 4:13).
- Good, better, best. Never let it rest. 'Til your good is better and your better gets best (St. Jerome).

Daddy reinforced her teachings, particularly with quizzes and instructions in practical applications.

I was born during World War II and lived in poverty-stricken Appalachia, but we always had enough and some to spare. Somehow, with God's grace, we never had to get in soup lines or receive other government handouts. One day, we went to the neighboring town to buy groceries, and people were standing in a line. I asked my mother what they were doing, and she told me they were getting soup. I started pulling on her to get in line because I loved soup. It was then that she explained to me about poor people and how they didn't have food to eat. That event had a profound effect on my life, and my heart went out to those people. As I reflect on my life, I can see how my strong desire to help disadvantaged populations was ignited by that event.

As active Christians, we had Bible study at home, were taught to pray at meals and bedtime, and lived Christian ethical lives. We went to Sunday school and church every Sunday. In Coretta, we had one church, which had Methodist services every other Sunday and Baptist services every other Sunday.

Mother was Baptist, and Daddy was Methodist; therefore, the entire family attended church every Sunday.

I learned to love church at an early age, and I began to sing solos at age two. I used to follow our preacher, at his invitation, because he said I was a special child. I didn't know it then, but he was my pastoral mentor.

When I was in the fourth grade, we moved to Bluefield, West Virginia, and my church life expanded. The children were given the choice to attend the Baptist or the Methodist church. I chose the Baptist church because I wanted to attend church with Mother. All the other kids attended the Methodist church with Daddy. In addition to the weekly Sunday school and church, I participated in the junior missionary society, church camps, conferences, and vacation Bible school. I sang in the choir and participated in the junior usher board and all holiday pageants. In other words, whenever the church doors were opened and I was not in school, I was in church. I also remember writing plays that were performed by my classes in elementary school and painting landscapes. I accepted Christ as my Savior at age eight. The church did not usually allow children that young to make a profession of faith, but somehow the pastor gave consent, saying, "She is ready."

I began to have a recurring dream when I was in the fourth grade. I dreamed that I was traveling with a group of people who were all dressed in white. I was dressed in white also and had a white covering over my head. This dream recurred over and over, and I saw myself mature in the dream, getting older as the dream recurred. I didn't know what it meant, but it greatly affected me because it recurred over and over again, year after year.

YEARS 10–20

A very traumatic event in my life occurred when I was in the sixth grade; my older sister passed from cancer. She was the closest sister to me, and we did many things together. She was four years older than me. She looked out for me, taught me how to do many things, and even let me hang out with her friends on occasion. She had been sick and was treated for two years. She left Bluefield the day after Thanksgiving to go to the National Institutes of Health in Bethesda, Maryland, where she could get more specialized help, but she passed on Christmas Eve in Maryland. When she passed, it hurt my heart so badly that I told my mother after the funeral I wanted to die and go to heaven so I could be with her.

When I passed to the seventh grade, we were strongly encouraged to desegregate the all-White school. Our parents, the community, and the church were behind us. They explained that in many instances, the Black school got the outdated, secondhand books from the White school, and the lab equipment, gym equipment, playground area, and sports field were better in the White school. However, we had seen and heard the news about Little Rock and other places of violence over desegregation; so, it was a tough decision. Nevertheless, I, along with three other girls and one boy, entered the all-White school in the seventh grade. All of us were straight-A students and were recruited particularly for that reason. That seventh grade was uneventful, and school was good. The principal held an assembly the first day of school and told everyone we would have no violence—and all students were to be treated with respect. How he was able to take that stance and make it stick, I do not know, but it worked.

When I passed to the eighth grade, the school I attended was merged with another school; all students went to the other school, but things got worse. We experienced the same responses of desegregation as those that made the national news: ridiculed; called the N-word and other derogatory names; and told we were stupid despite the fact we were straight-A students. We were jeered, made fun of, and were the brunt of dirty jokes. We suffered violence as students threw bricks at us every day at recess. I received a head injury from rocks and required medical treatment. The students chased us, throwing rocks after school, until we reached the bridge that separated the White neighborhood from the Black neighborhood. Despite the horrible, racist, demeaning, and violent conditions, we still remained straight-A students. However, there were students and teachers who made concerted efforts to treat the Black students kindly and with helpfulness, although in the minority.

When I passed to the ninth grade, we moved to Toledo, Ohio, because the mines shut down, and my daddy took the family to Toledo, where we lived with his cousin. Dad found work and bought our first home. In Toledo, I joined Braden Methodist Episcopal Church. Those were the days when the Central Jurisdiction existed, but I didn't understand that it was the racist separation of Black people in the Methodist Church. It did not dawn on me until I was in seminary that the church also needed to be desegregated.

In high school, I expanded my involvement in church by teaching vacation Bible school and Sunday school, being active in the youth fellowship, and being a youth representative on the administrative board/council on ministries. I continued to sing in the choir, serve as usher, write plays, choreograph dances that were performed by the youth fellowship, and attend camps and conferences. As president of the youth fellowship, I accompanied our pastor to many district and conference events where I continued to grow in my love for God and mission work.

In high school, there was also segregation and discrimination, but it was toned down and not in the majority. However, in my first year, a Black girl was voted queen in my high school that was practically one-third Black students. The next day, when we arrived at school, there was a Black scarecrow hung from the ceiling with a noose around his neck. This gained city and statewide media attention.

Most of the teachers were wonderful, but some were discriminatory in overt and covert ways. For example, my English teacher, who also directed the high school plays, overtly treated the Black and White students alike. I was encouraged to be active in the drama club and enjoyed participating in the plays and dance routines that accompanied the drama. On the other hand, another teacher covertly tried to discourage me from taking the academic subjects necessary to qualify for a premed academic tract in college. She also told me I would never be accepted into medical school and should set my career goals on teaching. Medical schools were not accepting women then; therefore, I can somewhat understand why she tried to dissuade me and guide me into something more attainable. However, she was obviously prejudiced in trying to steer me to easy subjects. Fortunately, I was not dissuaded from the courses that would be in alignment with my career goals, and I did not change my career goals.

My recurring dream continued. When I was in the eleventh grade, I was driving down the street and saw a woman dressed in the same clothing and head covering as I had seen in my dream. I saw her going into a Catholic church. I parked the car and hurriedly went into the Catholic church. When I got in, there was no one there but the priest. I told him I had seen a woman come in the church and asked if he knew who she was.

He said, "Yes. That was Sister ..." (I don't remember the name he said).

I told him about seeing myself in dreams wearing the same outfit, and he explained that she was a nun. I asked what a nun was, and he explained that a nun dedicates her life to God and the ministry of the church. He further explained that they lived in a residence with other nuns, and they did not marry. Instantly, I thought, *Well, that is certainly not for me.* I thanked him, left the church, and never had the dream again.

I finished high school, entered a local college, and experienced a racist environment. So, I dropped out of school after the first year and entered the workforce. I was tired and fed up with being a trailblazer and fighting for equal rights in school systems.

YEARS 20–30

I worked as a dental receptionist, medical receptionist, optometrist receptionist, health insurance claims processor, and nurse aid. As my career goal was to be a doctor, I intentionally looked for health-related jobs while I took courses occasionally at the university to keep my mind academically in tune. After being out of school for several years, I entered Norfolk State University, a historical Black college, and I finished my undergraduate degree in biology with a minor in chemistry. While at Norfolk State, I continued high academics and directed the annual fundraising events, which gave me good experience in community organizing and networking. These skills would later prove to be advantageous when I served as pastor.

Martin Luther King Jr., before his assassination, was leading marches for racial equality, and marches were held in many places in protest against segregation practices. I participated in marches and protests in Norfolk after his assassination. During those times, I became committed to the nonviolent movement because it was aligned with my life experiences and with my faith beliefs. In my senior year of college, I was recruited by the University of Pittsburgh Dental School, changed my career goals from physician to dentist, and entered the University of Pittsburgh Dental School after graduation.

When I entered dental school, I was only the third Black woman. The first two Black women had entered in the class a year ahead of me. Well, here I was again—on the battlefield for racial equality—and now it had expanded to gender equality. My time in dental school was not traumatic at all. Universities were under mandate to admit minority students and women, and I had been actively recruited by the school. I was given a full academic scholarship that was renewed every year. In addition, the dean was an advocate for women—his sister was also a dentist—and he had advised all women, Black and White, in my class that he was there to facilitate our getting our doctorate, and if we had any trouble, to let him know. I had to request his help on a couple of occasions, and he kept his word.

I only experienced a few episodes of overt or covert racism. Furthermore, there were several Black dentists on the faculty, two Black lab technicians, two Black hygienists, and several Black staff members. All of them were supportive, encouraging, and coaches to us in their particular area of expertise. The dental students and medical students attended some of the same classes together, and Black students had close association with the Black medical students, faculty, and staff. The overall environment was positive and academically demanding.

During the second semester of my freshman year at dental school, I began to get a nudging to enter ministry. I ignored that initial nudging and continued to pursue my dental degree. During my sophomore year, we were assigned to go into poor communities to advocate for dental health care. I enjoyed those interactions with the people, but it was not long before I came to the conclusion that the people certainly needed better dental care—but many more desperately needed the Lord. The nudging to enter ministry advanced to a strong tug on the heart. Nevertheless, I still resisted and said no. I could not believe that God would take me through all I had been through—in desegregating schools and all the blood, sweat, and tears I had endured to maintain high academics in dental school—to call me out. I rationalized that I couldn't answer the call.

During my junior year, the call continued to get stronger, and I began to bargain with God, saying, "I will answer the call after I finish dental school, get a MA in public administration, get a job as administrator of a dental clinic, get married, and build my new house." It was my intent to do ministry part-time while I kept a full-time job. That way, I could have the best of both worlds. God wasn't impressed with my deal, and the call continued to intensify until it was on my mind all the time. I couldn't sleep without being interrupted by the call, and my appetite was greatly affected. Internally, I was a wreck, but externally, I was described as "got the world on a string, sitting on a rainbow."

By the time I entered my senior year, I was completing my requirements for graduation and making plans for admission into the Graduate School of Public Health at the University of Pittsburgh where I would earn a Master of Arts in public administration. This would qualify me to serve as an administrator in a dental clinic in addition to practicing dentistry. Simultaneously, the call to enter ministry was very, very loud and unrelenting. Again, I continued to rationalize. I thought, *I don't know any full-time women ministers in any capacity, and I don't want to be a trailblazer for women in the church. I've had enough of trailblazing!*

Besides, pastors don't make enough money for the lifestyle I envisioned with a fabulous new home, a yacht, luxury cars, world travel, a private plane, and all the other expensive trimmings that were possessed by dentists I knew in the Pittsburgh area.

I continued to say no, but I was getting worn out in the struggle of saying no to God. Oh, let me also mention that I was in a tremendous faith struggle because God had been so good to me, had blessed me throughout the years, and had worked miracles in my life, family, and other loved ones, and now I was saying no to the *one thing* that God had asked me to do for Him. To ease my conscious, I began to get more intensely involved in my church. I developed numerous outreach programs and conducted community fairs for the church, but the struggle continued.

In October of my senior year, 1974, I was awakened in the middle of the night with excruciating pain. Pain was not part of my norm. I was very healthy, had healthy nutritional eating habits, exercised regularly, lived a healthy lifestyle, and had annual checkups. I knew something was drastically wrong. I went to my physician when his office opened the next day, only to be told that I had an abdominal tumor and needed to have surgery immediately. In a flash, I recalled the three major options of surgery: good surgery with no complications and a favorable prognosis; surgery with complications resulting in varied impairments of functions; and death. I immediately thought, *what if I have complications and cannot function enough to ever answer the call—or worse yet, I die on the table and go into eternity with a no on my lips to God.* I couldn't bear the thought of either of those outcomes, and I said to the doctor, "I can't have the surgery now. I am here without family, and I need to have time to gather family so I will have someone to care for me while I convalesce. I also want to finish this semester because it is too late to get my money back if I drop my classes. I don't want to have surgery and be incapacitated over the Thanksgiving, Christmas, and New Year holidays."

The doctor hit the roof and tried to dissuade me from postponing the surgery, but to no avail. So, since he couldn't force me, he made a deal with me that I was to come to his office weekly and get examined to see if there was unusual growth. If there was, I would agree to have surgery immediately. I agreed, but I did not express to him the most important reason for postponing the surgery; it was to give me time to talk with the Lord, get specific instructions, clarity, and guidance on the call to ministry. I had previously been so busy resisting and saying no that the particulars of the call had not been revealed to me.

I left the doctor's office and went home to engage in a prayer-fast to seek God's face and get directions. I began the fast with a prayer to hear from the Lord and a resolve to be obedient and follow God. I vowed to fast until I heard from God. I prayed scriptures, sang songs, meditated, and lay prostrate before the Lord. On the third night, God opened my eyes and showed me that I had entered dental school with the godly idea of helping people to have a better life through dental health care.

However, somewhere along the way, my motives had become polluted—and now my primary motivation was materialistic. In addition, my pursuit of material things had surpassed my love for Him. Therefore, I was worshiping false gods and not the true and living God. I was horrified at the condition of my heart. I repented, and I cried out to God in sorrow and shame, asking for forgiveness. I envisioned myself as the "prodigal" daughter who had been feeding pigs and wallowing in the pigpen.

At that moment, I felt an overwhelming envelopment of God's love and forgiveness filling every fiber of my being and holding me close. It was so close that I could hear the heartbeat of God as he called me to go and tell the world of his amazing, unconditional love while establishing a Christian community outreach center. Simultaneously,

I felt an overwhelming burden lifted from my heart. I experienced feelings of being reconnected, protected, and selected.

I fell in love with Jesus all over again, and I knew this love was a deeper love than I had been capable of before. I ended the fast happy, joyful, and full of excitement, thinking that despite all my messy rejections, pride, and arrogance, Jesus still loved me and wanted me to tell His Gospel story and to let others know that His love, mercy, and salvation were real. I could also add my own story of personal experiences to the Gospel story in the Bible. I was now experiencing a new beginning as well as a new birth at another dimension of spiritual growth.

The next morning, I went to the dean of the dental school and told him I was going into the ministry and would be withdrawing from school. Surprisingly, he was very sympathetic because he had a brother who was a priest and had seen what his brother went through in answering the call. However, he did not allow me to withdraw. Instead, he granted me a leave of absence—and he made me promise that I would return and finish those last six months and get my degree at some point in time. When I made that promise, I thought I could do that, but in hindsight, it didn't materialize.

The first phase of my call was to establish a Christian outreach center, and I immediately began that process in October 1974. Things went well. I prepared the plans for the establishment of the outreach center, and I started working on fundraising. I was faithful every week in going to my doctor's office for examination.

During the Christmas break, I went to Toledo to inform my family that I was to have surgery on January 3. We began to strategize how they could be supportive of me during the surgery and recovery process. They knew I would be out of school, probably for the last semester of my senior year, but they assumed I would return to school in the fall of 1975 to finish. Then I dropped the bomb on them and said, "I have already withdrawn from school, and I will not be returning because I am answering the call to ministry."

My family pointed out that I had been through too much to get to the end and quit. They were heartbroken because I would have been the first doctor in our bloodline, and our family was so looking forward to that achievement. They recalled all the barriers I had broken in my lifetime in educational systems not to cross the finish line. Furthermore, they asked if I knew how many people had been supportive of me and how disappointed they would be. My mother and one sister agreed with all the above rationale, but they encouraged me to follow my heart. It was a tremendously emotional, heartbreaking event on my side and theirs.

Returning to Pittsburgh, I continued to go to the doctor's office for my weekly examinations. On New Year's Eve 1974, I went to a Pentecostal church for a watch night service. After the sermon was over, the pastor gave an invitation for anyone who needed a healing to come forth so the elders could anoint with oil, lay hands, and pray for a healing. I immediately rushed to the altar, but when I got there, the altar was full. When the elders got to me, they anointed me with oil, laid hands on me, and began to pray. I felt what seemed like an electric current traversing from the crown of my head to the sole of my feet. The power was so overwhelming that I fainted and fell on the floor. When I awakened, I knew I was healed.

On January 2, 1975, I was scheduled to go for my pre-op exam in preparation for surgery on January 3. When the doctor examined my abdomen, he found nothing. Bear in mind that I had been keeping my weekly exams; suddenly, there was no tumor. The doctor was puzzled, and then I told him what had happened in church on New Year's Eve. He wasn't convinced that a miracle healing had taken place, and he ordered more tests. Further tests revealed no tumor. A miracle healing had occurred.

YEARS 30–31

I continued to work on the plans for the outreach center, and by April, I was involved in the funding stage. Then, in May 1975, I received the second phase of my call to ministry.

I went to Toledo for Mother's Day, and while I was in worship at Braden UMC, I heard an audible voice telling me, "I want you to preach!" I wasn't certain if it was God. I told my brother who was an ordained minister, inquiring what I should do. He advised that I should pray about it and ask God for guidance and God would show me (with a smile on his face and a little chuckle).

That evening, as I was on my knees doing my night devotions, I received a vision from God, and it was very plain. Jesus said to me again, "I want you to preach!" I was sure that it was the Lord, and the next day, I called Pittsburgh Theological Seminary and began the admissions process. In the meantime, I completed the plans for the outreach center and turned the project over to the pastor of the church for implementation. I enrolled in the Master of Divinity program in the fall of 1975.

Songs that were formative in my life in the previous events:

Many songs were formative in my life, but the most influential was "Just Look for Me in Heaven Somewhere." This song was taught to me, and I was told that at age two, I crawled under the casket of my grandmother and sang that song, impromptu, and to my mother's horror (she was afraid I would turn the casket over). I loved that song, and it was very meaningful to me and still is. "Amazing Grace," "Love Lifted Me," and "I'd Rather Have Jesus" were songs that flooded my soul when I was in the prayer-fast and said yes to the call to ministry.

2. Recall the people who significantly contributed to your Christian formation up to the acceptance of the call. Tell the stories of how they influenced your life.

My mother and daddy taught me about Christ and Christian living by precept and example. My parents taught us that we were blessed by God and that God provided for our needs miraculously. They would point out how God provided for our family despite the fact that others around us were living in poverty. They quoted scriptures in association with life events so we could make spiritual connections in our lives. They taught us to memorize scriptures and to use them for guidance in our daily living. They took us to church and taught us to be active in the life of the church, while they themselves attended Sunday school, church, United Methodist Men, and missionary society, and they were officers in the church and on committees. They taught us to pray, and they were prayer warriors. They were careful to point out the hand of God in our daily lives in ordinary and in miraculous ways.

My Baptist pastor in Caretta, West Virginia, became my pastoral mentor, allowing me to shadow him on Sundays. I learned to love the pastor, and I enjoyed learning what pastors do.

My first/second/third grade teacher—I attended a one-room school, and she taught grades one through three—became my Christian role model. She was such a loving Christian lady, and she included reading of the Bible and praying in the everyday curriculum. She enhanced my love for Christ and education that had been instilled by my parents. I was her favorite student, and she remained my favorite teacher—only to be rivaled by my botany professor at Norfolk State and my Christian education director at the Methodist Theological Seminary in Ohio (incidentally, all Black women).

My pastor of Central Baptist Church in Bluefield had great influence on my spiritual formation, and it was under his leadership that I was again encouraged to be active in the full life of the church. I learned by participation that faith in God was the door by which one was active in the ministries of the church as well as worship. He was encouraging of my participation in all ministries and age-appropriate activities. He also was supportive of me when I gave my heart to Jesus at age eight.

I attended the Baptist church, and the pastor of the John Wesley Methodist Episcopal Church in Bluefield, West Virginia, also had great influence on my formation. He was instrumental in leading the churches and community to support the Black students when we desegregated the schools, giving spiritual, moral, and physical support. He embodied believing in Jesus and living the Christian faith in everyday life, especially while advocating social justice.

In Toledo, my cousin and her husband, who was a pastor, were great influences. They were very benevolent, charitable, and loving people. Their acts of charity were inclusive of extended family, members of the church, members of the community, and strangers. My concept of loving and serving God continued to expand while living with them, and for the rest of the years of their lives.

At Braden Methodist Episcopal Church in Toledo, my pastor was instrumental in allowing me to get involved in leadership roles as youth president, youth representative on the administrative council, Sunday school teacher, and as a vacation Bible school teacher. He also taught me many things about the Methodist church, pastoral relationships, and involvement in the church in the Central Jurisdiction. As I traveled throughout Ohio with him to various meetings, conferences, and camps, I continued to grow in my love for Christ and the church.

Later, another pastor at Braden Church was helpful in teaching me about outreach ministry and the role of social justice in the church. He was instrumental in helping the youth get involved in civil rights marches and protests in Toledo. He taught us that standing for human rights was essential to our faith in Jesus Christ, who also stood for social justice. He also greatly influenced my deepening in my prayer life during prayer and Bible study classes.

A youth adviser at Braden had a profound effect on my spiritual growth as well. She took me under her wings, and I experienced unconditional love from her. She was supportive of me in church activities, and her love extended to being supportive of me in school activities as well. I had such a fond and loving relationship with her that she became like a surrogate mother to me.

In dental school, one of the Black lab technicians was also the pastor of a Pentecostal church, and I started attending the church at his invitation. I never left my Methodist roots, but I was convinced in my heart that God was not so concerned with what denomination or church affiliation one had as with the condition of one's heart and the sincerity of worship. He was the pastor who invited me to attend watch night service at another Pentecostal church where I received my miracle healing, although he was not the one who preached the sermon. Under his leadership, I learned to fast and tithe. These disciplines I continue even today.

While in dental school, there were two women who loved me and became my "moms" away from home. I lived with one, and the other one lived next door. I cannot describe how these two women cared for me as if I were their daughter. They cooked meals for me daily, bought me clothes and other gifts, celebrated holidays and birthdays, and encouraged me when I was having a hard time with my courses. They just "loved on me."

3. Recall the people/events that significantly served to deter your affirming the call to ordained ministry.

I was the only one who deterred my call. I did not share it with anyone until I had answered yes to the call to ministry. I did not understand the call to ministry, which was the first phase of my call, as a call to ordained ministry, although I understood later that there are many forms of ordained ministry and that outreach ministry can also be a form of ordained ministry.

4. When you received the call to ordained ministry, did you respond yes immediately and take appropriate action? Why or why not?

The first phase of the call was to community ministry, and I resisted that call for three years.

When I received the call to ordained ministry, it was the second phase of my call. I understood at the time that the call to preach was the call to ordained ministry, and I responded to that call the next day.

5. What was your occupation when you received the call, and what effect did it have on your response?

I was a freshman in dental school, studying to be a dentist, when I first received the call. It had a negative effect on my saying yes because I believed that I was following my chosen career as a dentist and ministry was something that I anticipated would be a part of my everyday life as a believer but was not my career path.

When I received the call to preach, I was engaged in the outreach ministry of the church. I had withdrawn from dental school, fully surrendered to God's will, and had already made a lifetime commitment to be obedient and follow Jesus wherever He would lead.

Saying yes when I received the call to preach was an easy transition because I was already following God in outreach ministry.

6. If you did not take immediate action to the call, recall the thinking/ rationale that caused resistance to your immediate response.

First, my rationale was: "It can't be God." As the call kept coming, my thinking was I can answer the call on the side, while still pursing and fulfilling my career choice as a dentist. I rationalized that I needed to make a certain income in order to have financial freedom and to be able to live the lifestyle I had chosen. Much of my thinking was intertwined with my beliefs in rising above racism and oppression as a Black woman. After all, I had spent most of my life fighting for equality, and the income as a dentist would help level the playing field while at the same time I would be a living example for others who would follow in my footsteps in fighting for justice, equality, and equity in academic fields of study.

7. What occurred that enabled you to overcome the resistance to answering the call?

Diagnosis of a tumor and the revelation of my worshipping false idols (material possessions) during a prayer-fast enabled me to have a willingness to say yes to the call. I said yes to outreach ministry first— and then I said yes to preach when that call came several months later.

8. What was the time frame between receiving the call and saying yes with appropriate action?

It took three years to say yes to the call for outreach ministry. It only took one day to respond yes to the call to preach.

9. *What role did the church play in your answering or not answering the call immediately?*

The church played no direct role in my answering or not answering the call immediately. The church was not aware of the call.

10. *Were there any spiritual disciplines that played a role in your resistance or acceptance of the call? Tell the stories.*

The spiritual disciplines of prayer and fasting played a tremendously significant role in my acceptance of the call to the outreach ministry. During a three-day absolute fast, I received revelations of my corrupted heart (love of the world) and my worship of false idols (dental career and materialism) that led to my repentance and receiving of love and forgiveness from Almighty God. My prayer-fast always included the disciplines of reading scripture, meditation, and singing spiritual songs.

The discipline of worship played a profound role in my acceptance of the call to preach. It was during a worship service that I heard the voice of God say, "I want you to preach." As I pondered on this new call and direction, I discussed it with my brother, believing that God would confirm His word out of the mouth of two or three witnesses. Consequently, I was putting the discipline of memorized scripture into practice as I pondered this call. Then, I entered into my discipline of nightly prayer, and during the prayer time, I heard the voice of Jesus say again, "I want you to preach." Twice on the same day, I heard the audible voice of God: one during worship and one during prayer.

In summary, prayer, fasting, reading of scripture, meditation, singing spiritual songs, and worship played significant roles in my acceptance of the call.

11. *In retrospect, how do you see God's hand at work in your life that prepared you for ordained ministry?*

I can see God's hand at work in the lives and parenting of my parents, who taught me to love the Lord and live according to His purpose. All during my life, beginning at early childhood, God has placed pastors in my life who continued to expand my love for Jesus and, unconsciously to me, a love for ministry. I was exposed to every aspect of church life that was possible for my given age at various times in my life, which furthered my love for Christ and the church, from early childhood until I accepted the call. In addition, I can see the Lord was preparing my heart for ministry when I had the recurring dream seeing myself in a nun's habit.

12. When you accepted the call to ministry, what was the response from persons in your life?

The dean of the dental school was affirming and granted permission for me to take a leave of absence with the condition that I return later to finish my degree.

Initially, most of the family was opposed. My mother and one sister, when seeing my passion to answer the call, encouraged me to pursue what was on my heart. The rest of my immediate family became supportive by the time I entered seminary, except my daddy. Daddy did not have a change of heart until my second year in seminary, but he became one of my greatest advocates.

Students in my class, the dean, and my professors were very supportive. In fact, they all came with their wives—to my surprise—to my trial sermon. The church was packed.

PHASE 2

1. Tell the story of your first three years while meeting the requirements necessary for elder's or deacon's ordination or for local pastor's requirements. What were some of your struggles and victories as you pursued answering the call?

- *Share your stories with the Board(s) of Ordained Ministry. In what ways were they helpful? Did you have any identifiable issues that you were told to improve upon?*
- *If you were assigned to a church(s) during those first three years, what relationships did you have with the parishioners and the community?*
- *When you attended seminary or licensing school, what were your experiences with faculty, staff, and peers? Include the specific years.*

I answered the call to ministry in 1975 while I was a watch-care member in a Black Pentecostal Church. The Pentecostal bishop of that area indicated he did not ordain women as pastors. Since I was still an official member of the United Methodist Church, I decided to pursue the steps to ordination in the United Methodist Church.

I began the process by enrolling at Pittsburgh Theological Seminary (PTS), a Presbyterian seminary, in Pittsburgh, Pennsylvania, in August 1975 as a Master of Divinity student. I received full tuition scholarship, but I had to work to cover my living expenses. Shortly thereafter, I was assigned as a student intern to a Black UMC. My ministerial duties were well received, and it was a good placement.

In November 1976, I went before the SPRC to obtain their approval for entry into the process for ordained ministry. The meeting was highly emotionally charged; there were seven members plus the pastor who were adamantly in favor of my approval, and there were two members who were adamantly against my approval. The two who voted against me did not state any reason for disapproval other than the fact that they did not believe in women pastors.

The vote was taken, and the result was eight in favor and two not in favor. I was approved to continue the process for ordained ministry; however, the two opposing members took hostile actions in the continuing process that resulted in preventing me from continuing in the UMC. I had no recourse but to leave the United Methodist denomination. I was assigned an internship at an AME church and I was received warmly by the pastor and congregation.

Unfortunately, there developed some irreconcilable issues with the pastor, and I was then assigned to an internship at an AMEZ church.

While I was serving as student intern at the AMEZ church, I applied for a secretarial position with the AMEZ bishop, and I got the position. Working closely with the AMEZ bishop, I was encouraged to join that denomination. I was warmly received by the pastor and congregation. The bishop and his wife were very supportive, kind, and gracious. My service at the AMEZ church was affirming, supportive, and encouraging.

In the winter of 1998, the seminary changed the criteria for scholarships, beginning in the fall of 1999. I met the academic qualifications—but not some of the other criteria. I did not have the financial resources to continue without the scholarships I was receiving from Presbyterian sources.

With the different denominational moves and the pending discontinuance of scholarship funds, I changed my major from a MDiv to a Master of Arts in religion, and I began to work on my thesis so that I could graduate with a degree that year.

The Board of Ordained Ministry interviews at the AMEZ denomination were affirming of my continuance with ordained ministry.

My seminary experiences at Pittsburgh Theological Seminary were very positive. The professors and staff were encouraging and supportive. The dean and I became friends while I worked as a student typist in his office, and he took me under his wing, becoming my mentor. Our friendship expanded as I also related to him when I was the president of the Black Student Organization. My seminary life experiences were lifeblood for me as I went through several traumatic sexist experiences in pursuit of ordained ministry.

I graduated debt-free with an MA in religion in 1999 from Pittsburgh Theological Seminary.

The AMEZ bishop held a special conference at the AMEZ church where I was an attending so that I could receive my deacon's ordination and accept a position that was offered to me from the Virginia Conference UMC where I would serve, on loan, as a part-time pastor of a UMC Church in Palmyra, Virginia, and part-time director of a UMC outreach mission in Charlottesville, Virginia. It was my intention to work until I could enroll and receive a scholarship at another seminary or earn enough money to pay my tuition and expenses to complete my MDiv.

The outreach mission was specifically designed to reach out to the Black community and provide a variety of spiritual, academic, and recreational activities. The outreach mission was successful over the summer because the activities were held in a local park. When the weather changed, the activities were held at the White church where my office was located, but the Black children refused to go there.

The grant for the outreach mission position was discontinued after a year, and I returned to Pittsburgh. I worked as a medical receptionist at a hospital. Realizing that it would take an eternity to save enough money on that salary, I moved back home to Toledo where I found a better-paying job and could save more money living with my parents.

In 1981, I was introduced to the admissions recruiter at the Methodist Theological Seminary in Ohio (MTSO) by the pastor of my home church, Braden UMC. I was offered a full-time scholarship. I supplemented my scholarships with work-study and later as a student pastor of Richards Chapel UMC in Troy, Ohio.

My life and experiences at MTSO were also exceptionally wonderful. The president, faculty, and staff were very good to all the students, and there were no differences between the treatment of the male and female students. The professors were so outstanding that it is hard to single out anyone except the White professor who encouraged me to pursue a PhD and a Black professor who taught me a lot about Martin Luther King Jr. and his endeavors from a Christian ethics point of view.

At MTSO, the Black director of field education was exceptionally encouraging to Black women students. She introduced me to a number of scholarship funds for ethnic students, which I received, and she facilitated funding for students to attend several national conferences. There was either a fire or some water damage in the dormitory where I lived (I can't remember which). The director was so kind that she invited four women students to her home where we stayed for a few weeks until the damage was repaired. She was so kind, and she certainly went above and beyond the call of duty.

I was elected as the president of the Black Seminarians organization, and we strongly advocated for specific classes in spiritual formation. We were told initially that spiritual formation was inherent in all courses. We did not accept that answer because we knew spiritual formation needed to be offered as courses, the same as all other subjects. We kept advocating for spiritual formation classes until the administration responded affirmatively and hired a Catholic nun to teach spiritual formation. They could not find a Protestant professor because, at that time, other Protestant seminaries were not offering training in spiritual formation either.

I graduated from MTSO in 1984 with an MDiv, debt-free.

I was ordained an ordained elder being one of two Black women to be the first Black clergywomen ordained as elders in the West Ohio Conference in 1986.

2. Share your stories of each individual appointment since beginning the process for ordination until 2016. Include the following:

- *What lessons did you learn from each appointment?*
- *What meaningful relationships were established? Include personal, professional, and church member relationships.*
- *What was your personal and church financial state?*
- *Relate any successes or challenges you faced in each appointment. Were there any personal events that affected your ministry (weddings, deaths, or illnesses?)*
- *What Methodist, national, local, or world events affected your appointments? Explain how.*
- *Have any of the meaningful relationships established with your parishioners been continued over the years?*

I served in the following appointments during my forty years before retirement as follows:

- Haden's Chapel UMC, Palmyra, Virginia, and Methodist Outreach Mission, Charlottesville, Virginia.
- Richards Chapel UMC: Troy, Ohio.
- Appointed to Attend School.
- New Life UMC: North Braddock, Pennsylvania.
- McMasters UMC: Turtle Creek, Pennsylvania.
- McMasters UMC: Turtle Creek, Pennsylvania and Western Pennsylvania Conference Staff: Cranberry Township, Pennsylvania.
- Western Pennsylvania Conference Staff: Cranberry Township, Pennsylvania.
- Western Pennsylvania Conference Staff: Cranberry Township and Career Exploration Mission: Washington, Pennsylvania.
- Career Exploration Mission: Washington, Pennsylvania and Buena Vista UMC: Pittsburgh, Pennsylvania.
- Career Exploration Mission: Washington, Pennsylvania.
- McMasters UMC: Turtle Creek, Pennsylvania.
- Emory UMC: Pittsburgh, Pennsylvania.
- Coraopolis UMC: Coraopolis, Pennsylvania.
- United Theological Seminary: Dayton, Ohio.
- First UMC: Bridgeville, Pennsylvania.
- Port Vue UMC: Port Vue, Pennsylvania.

FIRST APPOINTMENT:
1979–1980, PART-TIME PASTOR, HADEN'S CHAPEL, PALMYRA, VIRGINIA; PART-TIME DIRECTOR, METHODIST OUTREACH MISSION, CHARLOTTESVILLE, VIRGINIA

Haden's Chapel was a small Black rural church, which consisted of approximately three families. Worship attendance was fifteen or twenty people. I was their first clergywoman pastor. The members were very dedicated and sincere in their commitment to Christ and the church. The members were warm and welcoming with a lot of family history that dated back a couple of generations. The families lived in the rural area with the closest city being Charlottesville. I was there for a year, and during that time, we started a choir. Despite their small size, they were active in district and conference events. My tenure there was memorable, and the members treated me graciously as their first woman pastor.

The Methodist Outreach Mission was a ministry designed to reach unchurched Black children in the Charlottesville area. As a new ministry, the groundwork had to be laid, and there was no Black UMC in the area. My office was located in a White UM church. We had begun to get good attendance at the program during the summer because it was held at a local park. Winter programs were scheduled at the White church, but the children would not attend there. After failed attempts to get the Black children to come to the church, the funding for the outreach was discontinued after the first year, and I returned to Pittsburgh.

SECOND APPOINTMENT:
RICHARD'S CHAPEL UMC, TROY OHIO, 1983– 1987, STUDENT PASTOR THEN PASTOR

I was appointed to Richard's Chapel as a student pastor in 1983, and when I graduated from seminary in 1984, I was appointed pastor. I was their first clergywoman pastor. It was a good appointment. The church was a small membership Black congregation that was very active, and during my appointment, it increased in ministries, membership, and finances. We were engaged in community events and in district and conference activities. In addition, we engaged in Black ecumenical ministries as well as ministries with the Troy Council of Churches. We also developed two creative after-school programs and conducted a successful capital campaign.

I learned that small-membership churches could have vital ministries and serve the needs of the community when there is clear vision, an engaging pastor, a hardworking congregation, and intentionality in leadership development.

Meaningful relationships were established with many of the parishioners, especially the secretary, president of the UMW, the children's director, the youth director, and her husband. All of them were very supportive and were skillful and caring leaders in a variety of roles. We became friends and socialized together in non-church activities as well.

The church moved from equitable salary support to paying my salary as full-time pastor. I was a single pastor with no debt, and the salary was slightly above minimal salary, but I managed it well.

There were no personal events that affected my ministry or Methodist, national, or world events that affected the ministry.

My friends and I continued to communicate after I left Troy. While I was pastoring in Pittsburgh, the son of the youth director came to live with me for several months in an effort to get his life back on track. The youth director later became a nondenominational pastor, and I ordained her. She and her husband remain friends today, and we communicate via email, text, and phone. Several others kept contact until they passed.

Third Appointment:
attend school at Duquesne University,
Pittsburgh, Pennsylvania, 1987–1991

I began school at the Institute of Formative Spirituality of Duquesne University, a Catholic private school in 1987. Originally, the program was opened to Catholics only, but they had recently opened the program to Protestants as well. It required enrollment in the Institute's Master's program first, followed by a separate admissions process for the PhD program.

I was well received, as an ordained clergywoman, by the students and professors despite the fact that Catholics do not ordain women.

I became friends with several of the professors, men and women. In fact, two of the professors came to me and asked me to pray with them privately for their healing with the laying on of hands and use of anointing oil. One professor was instantly delivered from smoking, and the other was scheduled for surgery, and the surgery was miraculously not needed. We remained in contact for several years after my graduation from the PhD program. My friendship with several students remained after graduation, and I remained in contact with two of the students until 2015 when I retired and moved to Toledo. We would meet occasionally for lunch, visit each other's homes, attend cultural activities, and keep abreast with each other's family occurrences. Now we communicate via phone and social media.

While a student at Duquesne, I started a liturgical dance group, consisting of nuns, priests, and other students in the program. I started the group because I needed to have some form of exercise during my day. I expected that lay Catholics would join, but I was surprised that nuns and priests also joined the group. Even more surprisingly, we were asked to dance at the institute's twenty-fifth anniversary celebration.

God moved in mysterious ways as friendships were established with my Catholic colleagues, and professors. I was especially surprised at the openness of the Catholic priests. Surprisingly, two of my friends who were Catholic priests were ushers in my wedding in 1990.

I graduated from Duquesne University in 1994 with a PhD. I received Catholic funds for tuition and fees, all the years of my attendance, and I supplemented my living income as part-time pastor.

I graduated from Duquesne University debt-free.

Fourth Appointment:
Pastor of New Life UMC, North Braddock,
Pennsylvania, 1988–1990

New Life was a Caucasian congregation located in a transitional neighborhood. As the community was becoming progressively African American, the congregation wanted to stay in the neighborhood, and minister to the African American population. They requested the DS to send an African American pastor. They wanted a full-time pastor, but I was sent as a part-time pastor while attending Duquesne University. I was their first African American pastor and first clergywoman. The congregation was a caring congregation, and friendships developed quickly.

We assessed the church situation after outreach and evangelism efforts received no response from the community, and we determined the church had too long a history of being "all White" to gain the confidence of the community as a church open to all people, plus there were numerous Black churches in the community. We prayed and fasted corporately many times and determined that we should merge with another congregation while we still had assets to bring to the table. We mutually agreed the Holy Spirit was leading us to merge with McMasters UMC in Turtle Creek.

New Life drafted guidelines by which we were willing to merge. The guidelines were carefully planned and included organizational structures, processes, and procedures for ministry, the condition of keeping both pastors with equal authority as co-pastors, salaries, benefit packages, and other particulars. The DS facilitated our meeting to discuss the merger, and it all went very smoothly.

The only hiccup was the agreement for me to be co-pastor was changed, and I was appointed as associate pastor instead. I did not know of the change until it was announced at the annual conference. Since everything else with the merger was going so extremely well, I decided I would let it go, rather than make a fuss where I would be front and center.

The finances at New Life were going reasonably well, especially since they moved from a full-time pastor to a part-time pastor upon my arrival. I could only serve as part-time due to school.

My finances for a part-time salary, along with my scholarships were adequate for my living expenses, and that salary was retained in the merger as agreed.

I learned that a White congregation could rise above racism and sexism to become the kind of church Christ has called us to be.

On a personal note, I married my husband in July 1990. He was a Baptist pastor. During the planning stages of the merger, I was also planning my wedding and attending school. Only with God's grace was I able to manage all three. The New Life congregation welcomed my husband and treated him with respect and love. The congregation gave us a wedding shower, and several members participated in the wedding, in a variety of roles. The church was excited about our wedding and treated us royally.

Meaningful relationships were established with several members of the church. These relationships were retained for many years after I left, and I was invited back to birthday, anniversary, and graduation parties. One member, who is now ninety-three years old, still sends me updates on her family and CDs of special events. We talk on the phone occasionally and send each other cards.

FIFTH APPOINTMENT:
ASSOCIATE PASTOR AT MCMASTERS UMC, TURTLE CREEK
UMC, TURTLE CREEK, PENNSYLVANIA, 1990–1992

The New Life congregation made the physical move and merged with the McMasters congregation, and all of the guidelines were mutually accepted. The New Life Congregation was well received and so was I as pastor. I was their first African American pastor and first clergywoman.

The finances of the merged church greatly improved with the combined assets of both churches. The New Life Church was sold, and the operational finances of New Life Church were transferred to McMasters. Eventually, the New Life parsonage was sold.

All ministry areas were combined and cochaired by a member of each church. The merger proceeded according to the premerger agreement, and the ministry proceeded very smoothly.

The salaries and benefit packages were retained the same as before the merger as agreed. I learned that mergers could work well when approached with specifics, careful planning, and desirability by both congregations.

My wedding occurred after one month of being the associate pastor at McMasters, and they too became excited about the wedding, welcomed my husband and me, and some of them participated in the wedding in a variety of ways. The congregation felt loved because we included them in the wedding. My husband and I felt so blessed to have two loving Anglo congregations, now merged, and both equally as loving toward us. The merged congregation gifted us with the wedding rehearsal dinner, and the entire wedding party of forty-one people was graciously embraced.

When I married my husband, a widower, I became a wife and mother of four adult children. Simultaneously, I became grandmother of eight. I became a wife, mother, and grandmother in one "I do." It only took two years for us to become a close-knit family, and we remain close today.

I developed many friendships at the merged McMasters congregation. We have maintained our friendship over the years. In like fashion, I became friends with the senior pastor and his wife, and it was good to work with them. One member of the church decided to enter the ministry, and he stated that God had used me to influence his decision. One child who was in the second grade when I arrived developed a special spiritual connection, and we stayed in touch until he graduated from college. He invited me to his birthday parties and graduations during those years. We lost touch when I moved to Ohio to take the position at United Seminary. One couple became friends, and each time I received a new appointment, they would come on my first Sunday to give me support over the years. They also became prayer partners and remained so until the husband passed, but the wife remains so even now.

The bishop who appointed me as associate pastor at McMasters became one of my biggest advocates and friends when I served on the conference staff and as the CEO of the CEM projects. God demonstrated through our deeply developing friendship that forgiveness and love are foundational attributes of Christianity, and when we give our hurts and wounds to God, good can be the end result. With God's grace, we developed a deep love and appreciation for each other that still remains.

SIXTH APPOINTMENT:
ASSOCIATE PASTOR, MCMASTERS UMC, TURTLE CREEK;
CHURCH CONSULTANT, WESTERN PENNSYLVANIA CONFERENCE,
CRANBERRY TOWNSHIP, PENNSYLVANIA, 1991–1992

I was appointed to serve half-time associate pastor at McMasters and half-time church consultant. I continued with the same responsibilities at McMasters.

I was the first African American clergywoman hired on the Western Pennsylvania Conference staff. It was my responsibility as church consultant to assess the strengths and weaknesses of congregations and to develop plans for those congregations to increase membership, reach out into the community, and improve finances. Conflict management was also in my portfolio. The conference ministry was rewarding, and I developed some new skills while in that position.

The conference director was very open and fair in his oversight of his staff. I was treated equally in my position as the other three pastors who were hired in equal positions at the same time. The conference director demonstrated appreciation for my work and facilitated training for all his staff. All of the conference staff were friendly, and the work environment was very pleasant.

The conference churches were very receptive of my leadership, and the consultations were successful when implemented as planned.

SEVENTH APPOINTMENT:
DIRECTOR OF MISSIONS AND OUTREACH, WESTERN PENNSYLVANIA
CONFERENCE, CRANBERRY TOWNSHIP, PENNSYLVANIA, 1992–1996

I became the full-time director of missions and outreach in 1992. In that capacity, I served conference churches who desired to engage in creative missions in their local communities. I still served under the same conference director, and my salary was the same as the other former church consultants whose titles and duties also changed.

Again, I was treated equally and respectfully on the conference staff, and meaningful relationships were continued with my colleagues and other conference staff.

I had written a mission project, Career Exploration Mission (CEM), for children and youth while I planned the outreach for the Pentecostal church prior to enrolling at PTS. It was a comprehensive after-school program for children, youth, and families, including homework assistance, tutoring, public speaking, fine and performing arts, job training, and other components. I copyrighted the model, and it was implemented in the Western Pennsylvania Conference. It successfully addressed the needs of conference churches that were experiencing lack of outreach to their respective communities. The Conference Council on Ministries voted to accept the model as a conference model with conference funding, and it was included in the conference budget.

The approval of the CEM project, with conference funding, was a historic event.

EIGHTH APPOINTMENT:
DIRECTOR OF MISSIONS AND OUTREACH, WESTERN PENNSYLVANIA CONFERENCE, CRANBERRY TOWNSHIP, PENNSYLVANIA; FOUNDER/CEO, CAREER EXPLORATION MISSION, WASHINGTON, PENNSYLVANIA, 1994–1996

My new appointment was as half-time director of outreach and missions for the Western Pennsylvania Annual Conference and half-time as founder/CEO of the Career Exploration Mission in Washington, Pennsylvania. As a new conference program, the initial year with CEM was spent developing a board of directors, networking with other conference and district ministries, networking with community agencies/boards, fundraising, and establishing the ministry as a nonprofit corporation.

Eventually, CEM ministries were established in three other cities and remained viable until staff funding couldn't match staffing needs (nine years.) Many professional friendships were made as I continued in the two half-time positions. I worked alongside four district superintendents while serving the CEM Projects from 1994–2003, and good relationships were established with all four.

NINTH APPOINTMENT:
FOUNDER/CEO, CAREER EXPLORATION MISSION,
CRANBERRY TOWNSHIP; PASTOR, BUENA VISTA UMC,
PITTSBURGH, PENNSYLVANIA, 1996–1998

The salary of the two half-time positions remained the same as the two previous half-time positions. The position as half-time pastor of Buena Vista UMC was a good appointment. I was their first clergywoman pastor. The congregation was a Black congregation in decline, but it was still somewhat viable. The congregation desired to reach out more into the community, and new ministries were implemented under my leadership, including the CEM project. New ministries began to emerge during the two years of my appointment, and many children and youth began to attend the church as a result of the CEM project.

Meaningful relationships were established, and there was socializing on a personal level with several church families. One particular couple with their four sons became my surrogate family, and they have remained friends with frequent contact until this day. In fact, each time I would be appointed to another church, they would attend that church as well. That family still keeps in contact, and the sons relate to me as "Momma Jo."

CEM students from the four cities were featured at several annual conferences, and district events to display their singing and dancing talent acquired at the after-school program. Fundraising efforts for the CEM project were very successful and enabled the project to become self-supporting. At this time, the conference funding was discontinued.

On a personal note, my daddy went to be with the Lord in June

1997, and my mother in September 1997. Daddy had been in declining health for over ten years, and his death was difficult but expected. Mother had a heart attack and died suddenly in her sleep. Losing her suddenly—and so close to Daddy's passing—left my siblings and me reeling and rocking. The bishop, DS, my clergy colleagues, the Buena Vista congregation, and conference laity friends were very supportive.

It was God's grace that saw me through. I found that returning to the duties of ministry was therapeutic on both occasions.

Tenth Appointment:
1998–2003, founder/CEO of Career Exploration Mission, Washington, Pennsylvania, 1998–2003

The CEM project continued to grow and expand in attendance, funding, and partnerships. The students improved in academics, were placed in jobs, and became the pride of the cities where they were located. As the CEM project continued to expand in services, it became increasingly easy to obtain funding for services.

In 2002, it was still fairly easy to raise funding for program services, but it became disproportionately difficult to raise funding for the expanded staff needed for the program services. In addition, I was becoming weary of fundraising as my primary duty. I did not feel that I was fulfilling my call as I understood it. My husband had been diagnosed with multiple sclerosis and was becoming increasingly disabled. With all the above factors, the CEM board of directors, the DS, and I mutually agreed to close the CEM programs—even though there was sufficient funding to underwrite all of the program services except staff. That was a very difficult decision, especially in light of the progress that occurred in the lives of the students and their families.

It was a very meaningful and exceptional ministry and reached out to more than five hundred students annually, and they made exceptional advances in academics, the performing arts, and job skills. Some of the graduates of the program became first-generation college students.

In my personal life, I was also going through difficult times. In the summer of 2001, my husband and I brought our two grandnephews to live with us from Detroit with the hope of adopting them. However, due to complications in processing the case, we were only able to keep them for nine months, and that caused a lot of brokenness in the children and in my husband and me.

The personal difficulty was compounded in December 2001 when my brother passed suddenly. It was a shock to the entire family, and we didn't know the cause of his death until the autopsy revealed an undiagnosed heart condition.

The combination of my husband's increased debilitation, the botched adoption process in May 2002, burying my brother in January 2002, and closing the CEM projects in 2002 were very difficult to handle emotionally and spiritually. It was only through God's grace and the fervent prayers of the righteous people in my life that I was able to carry on.

ELEVENTH APPOINTMENT:
INTERIM PASTOR, MCMASTERS UMC, TURTLE CREEK, PENNSYLVANIA, AUGUST 1999–OCTOBER 1999

I served in this capacity for three months—until another pastor could be appointed—while I was serving as full-time CEO of the CEM Project. The interim position was delightful, and I returned to the merged congregation that I served in its initial merger status. It was a return "home."

TWELFTH APPOINTMENT:
PASTOR, EMORY UMC, PITTSBURGH, PENNSYLVANIA, 2003–2005

I was appointed as the first African American and first clergywoman at the Emory Church, serving under the first Black clergywoman appointed as DS in the Western Pennsylvania Conference. It was a multicultural church in decline. It was a good appointment as far as developing relationships with the congregation, and we were able to see a slight decrease in the decline. We were able to forge partnerships for ministry with some community groups, and it was refreshing to see hope being reestablished as new ministries began to emerge. I was able to establish a mini version of the CEM project that focused on the senior population.

Financially, it was a lateral move again, and salary and benefits remained the same.

In 2004, my husband went to be with the Lord, and I was devastated. I only took a couple of weeks off and returned to the congregation with all pastoral duties in place. My return to ministry was therapeutic in my grief process as it had been when both my dad, mom, and brother made their transitions.

The bishop, DS, the Emory congregation, many clergy colleagues, and conference laity friends were very supportive during my bereavement, and their presence and prayers helped lighten the grief.

THIRTEENTH APPOINTMENT:
PASTOR OF CORAOPOLIS UMC, CORAOPOLIS, PENNSYLVANIA, 2005–2006

I was appointed as the first African American clergywoman to the Coraopolis UMC, a Caucasian congregation, in 2005. The congregation had thriving ministries for children, youth, and adults. These ministries continued to thrive under my leadership. A CEM after-school program and a program for college students were also initiated under my leadership. Both were highly successful.

The SPRC was very supportive and did all they could to defuse any church conflict. They worked with integrity and made decisions that were in alignment with the Bible and the social ethics of the UMC. I was encouraged by their leadership and support despite some antagonistic actions by a few of the members. I prayed without ceasing, and I was able to lovingly relate to those who were unloving to me. To God be the glory!

While serving at Coraopolis, I was approached by the president of United Theological Seminary (UTS) to consider coming to Dayton to serve as the director of doctoral studies. This was the second time I had been asked to serve as the director. The first time was while my husband was seriously ill, and I could not consider it at that time.

After prayer and fasting, I accepted the position of director of doctoral studies at UTS. The title was later changed to associate dean of doctoral studies.

The Coraopolis congregation was stable in finances, and my salary was increased above my previous salaries.

FOURTEENTH APPOINTMENT:

DIRECTOR OF DOCTORAL STUDIES, UNITED THEOLOGICAL
SEMINARY, DAYTON, OHIO, 2006–2009 (TITLE LATER
CHANGED TO ASSOCIATE DEAN OF DOCTORAL STUDIES)

The seminary environment was challenging, but it was a delightful place to work. The faculty, staff, and students were friendly, engaging, and creative.

The challenge was experienced as I arrived and discovered the seminary had encountered a drop in total enrollment in both the master's and doctoral programs, and the school was on probation with the Association of Theological Schools. My primary responsibilities had to be focused on correcting academic weaknesses and improving enrollment in the doctoral program.

My administrative skills, acquired through my years of ministry, were very helpful in facilitating strategies. I designed and implemented curriculum changes. In addition to administrative duties, I taught a spiritual formation class in the master's program and designed and recruited several new cohort groups and mentors for the doctoral program. My administrative skills were expanded as I conducted the necessary changes for more academic viability. My two excellent administrative assistants were very helpful in my acclimation to the seminary environment and helping, as appropriate, with the necessary changes.

The salary and benefit package were a significant increase from previous positions. Finances were adequate for my needs.

With God's grace and much hard work, we were able to remove all the weaknesses in the doctoral department, and when combined with improvements in other departments, it enabled removal of the probation status. In addition, enrollment had begun to improve. However, the entire seminary budget was in crisis, and drastic cuts had to be made.

In 2009, several positions were eliminated, and several others were reduced to part-time. My position was reduced to half-time, and that salary was not adequate for my needs. The seminary offered to keep me half-time while serving a church. No part-time church position was available in Western Ohio, and I did not want to commute from Dayton to Western Pennsylvania, so I requested to be reassigned full-time to a church in Western Pennsylvania.

Several lasting professional relationships were developed with faculty, staff, and students, and several are still maintained via calls and social media.

In addition to the friendships at the seminary, I became close personal friends with a bishop and his wife who were pastors at a nondenominational church. In fact, they co-officiated, along with a UM bishop at my "wedding to Christ" ceremony. They were also my prayer and fast partners and remain so until this day.

FIFTEENTH APPOINTMENT:
PASTOR, FIRST UMC, BRIDGEVILLE, PENNSYLVANIA, 2009–2011

I was appointed to the Bridgeville church in 2009. I was their first African American and first clergywoman. I was told by the DS that the church was in years of decline with dwindling finances, and the projection was it would be reduced to a part-time pastoral position within two years. Nevertheless, I went to the church with a resolve to do all I could to help the church make a turnaround.

I focused my attention on helping the congregation grow spiritually and retain all the current ministries. Prayer and Bible studies strengthened the congregation, especially as we ventured out in healing ministries and studies in the Holy Spirit.

We had a healing service for one of our members who had cancer, and we watched God do a miracle. Although he passed nine months later, we saw a change in his condition—and his pain was totally removed until the last few days of his life.

The congregation was warm and welcoming, and friendships began to form. Many persons reached out to me to make me feel at home as their pastor by inviting me to their homes, to lunch, to social outings, and the like.

Tragically, during this time, the LA Fitness shooting occurred, and one of my members was fatally shot. This was a tremendous tragedy for me, our church, and for the community. Our community lost several people, and more were wounded. The churches in the area came together to help the city mourn and begin recovery back to normal. Many prayer vigils, worship services, counseling services, and home visits were conducted. The residents of the city responded well to the initiatives that were offered under the combined leadership of the clergy. I was able to give key leadership in my church as well as the community. The pastoral leadership of the city made combined efforts to address mass mourning, anger, bewilderment, and other responses to grief compounded by the senseless killings. It was a tremendously difficult time, but God saw us through.

I was able to spend concerted time with the family of my deceased member and help them walk through difficult decisions regarding her teenage son. Concentrated ministry and specialized counseling were provided for the children of the church because the deceased member had been in children's ministry for years, and the children were having a difficult time processing her death.

Good relationships were continued or initiated.

Despite the visibly meaningful ministries under my leadership, some disgruntled members left the church. I learned that when I have done my best, and others are not satisfied, I have to give it to the Lord and keep doing what God has called me to do. In no church setting is there 100 percent satisfaction with any pastor. I learned in a deeper way that I couldn't please everyone, and my number one goal was to please God.

I remained at the church for another year, and the rest of the time was spent in meaningful ministries. The projection of the church going to a part-time pastor became reality.

The church finances were in severe decline when I arrived, and my salary was less than the previous pastor, but I was able to manage.

Several persons have continued as friends, and we communicate via phone or social media. While I was at Bridgeville, I became friends with several people. One gentleman was embarking on extending his involvement in ministry and was considering the possibility of becoming ordained later. I became his mentor. Those friendships have been retained through phone calls and times of prayer.

SIXTEENTH APPOINTMENT:
SENIOR PASTOR, PORT VUE UMC, PORT VUE, PENNSYLVANIA, 2011–2015

I was appointed as senior pastor with an associate pastor who had been at the church for a long time. I was their first African American clergywoman. The associate pastor, a White clergywoman, was very helpful in my getting acclimated to the congregation and ministries. We worked very well together, and a good relationship emerged.

The church at Port Vue was a very active church with viable ministries for children, youth, and adults.

I found the congregation to be very loving, and welcoming to me, and many good relationships were developed within the congregation and community. However, there was brokenness in the church when I arrived due to some previous conflict. I was intentional in emphasizing and supporting spiritual growth ministries, which also assisted in the healing process. I saw some improvement with the brokenness, and the congregation began to heal.

The congregation increased in attendance, but the finances were fluctuating. We worked on improving the finances, but they continued to fluctuate with several major building needs that continued to emerge. Nevertheless, we were able to expand ministries and initiate new ones.

Unfortunately, tragedy struck at this appointment also. One of my teen members, a very beloved youth in our church, was found strangled with a belt at her home. Her death was a shock and extremely painful. She had served as an usher in church that same Sunday. Wow! I had grown to love that young lady because I had been working with the family for a while due to her sick brother. It was my first time having to eulogize a teen, and the questionable death made it even harder. Some said she was bullied at school, some said she was participating in an internet daredevil stunt, but nobody really knew. So again, I had to engage in giving comfort to the family, the community, and to the school's students, faculty, and staff. My experiences at Bridgeville helped in giving me insight for ministering to the family, church, and community, but it didn't make it any easier.

I found again that there are times that will occur when God is all you have, and God is all you need. The clergy and churches in the area offered support, but the major responsibility fell on me as the pastor of the young girl. In some ways, I believe we are all still in recovery over her death. Perhaps deeper healing will come at another time.

I have remained friends with many of the parishioners and with the associate pastor. We communicate by phone, email, and social media. Many of us still exchange birthday cards and Christmas cards with pictures of loved ones and letters. Several are prayer partners.

In Western Pennsylvania, I have had meaningful professional relationships with three bishops, several DSs, and several clergy colleagues.

I must also mention that one pastor and one layperson of other denominations who befriended me have remained friends, and we communicate with one other on a regular basis. The other Black clergywoman who was ordained elder at the same time as I was in West Ohio was later elected bishop, and she has remained a friend, confidant, and prayer partner over these years as well.

3. *Do you see any of your life stories depicted in the lives of the saints in the Bible? Was it helpful to see yourself in scripture as you journeyed in your appointments?*

I see my life story in the life of Joseph in the Old Testament. I was named after Joseph when my father named me Josephine. It has been helpful for me to keep my eyes focused on being who God has called me to be—even when injustices have occurred in my life. The story helps me refrain from revenge and to remember that even when others do evil against me, God means it for my good. While I am going through pain and hurt inflicted by others, I am able to seek the Lord and ask for God to show me some good, even in the midst of the struggle, and this approach keeps me spiritually grounded.

I relate to Paul on the road to Damascus. He was knocked off his high horse and was able to see that he was on the wrong path. I see myself as being knocked off my high horse when I was resisting the call on my life in dental school and saying no to God. Although I wasn't persecuting the Christians, my disobedience was just as bad.

I also see myself as Jonah running away from God and ending up in the belly of a whale. My whale manifested itself as an abdominal tumor. Like Jonah, I was released from the tumor after I became obedient and answered the call to ministry.

Finally, I see myself in the life of King Jehoshaphat who worshiped, prayed, and fasted when he faced the enemy, and that is what I do when I find myself in conflict, injustice, or other struggles. I receive strength and guidance through worship, prayer, and fasting. In addition, I further identify with King Jehoshaphat being given the direction to face the enemy with praise.

I have found that praise is a powerful weapon at any time—in addition to worship, prayer, fasting, and Bible study. I have seen God move in miraculous ways when I engage in those spiritual disciplines.

4. If you were the first Black woman, or among the firsts, in any of your appointments, state those firsts, and tell the stories. What words of wisdom would you pass on to others who may become pioneers during their ministry?

I was the first Black clergywoman appointed in all my church and extension ministry appointments

- One of two Black women to be first ordained in the West Ohio Conference in 1986.
- The first Black clergywoman appointed to Haden's Chapel UMC, Richard's Chapel UMC, and Buena Vista UMC (three Black churches.)
- The first Black clergywoman appointed to New Life, McMasters, Coraopolis UMC, Bridgeville First, and Port Vue United Methodist Churches (five Caucasian churches.)
- The first Black clergywoman appointed to Emory UMC (a multiracial church.)
- The first Black clergywoman appointed on the conference staff of the Western Pennsylvania UMC Annual Conference.
- The first Black UM clergywoman to serve as director and associate dean of United Theological Seminary.

What words of wisdom would you pass on to others who may become pioneers during their ministry?

- Keep the spiritual disciplines foremost in your life so that you will maintain your spiritual connection with God.
- Develop and/or keep personal friends beyond your congregation and beyond the UMC.

- Go to the assigned appointments with a cheerful heart, knowing that the bishop appoints—but God sends.
- Strive to be the embodiment of a loving and forgiving person.
- Do not carry grudges.
- Be a friend to others, and others will befriend you—even in environments of conflict.
- Look for the good in others—even those who do evil against you.

5. *In hindsight, how could the annual conference and/or other UM personnel be more helpful when assigning Black clergywomen as firsts in a given area of ministry?*

- it would be most helpful for the bishop and cabinet to be supportive of the Black clergywoman with specific plans for support, prior to the appointment.
- It would be helpful to have met the SPRC and congregations prior to the appointments to address ways to overcome racism that would probably occur.
- It would be helpful to track and document successful first appointments to assist in the appointments of future Black clergywomen who would be appointed as firsts in their areas of ministry.
- In addition, it would be helpful for the bishop and cabinet to specifically strategize when conflict had occurred prior to the appointment that was centered around the appointment of the Black clergywoman.
- Appointments to churches that pay more than minimal salary—and who have enough viability to retain a full-time pastor over a period of time—would be helpful.
- I am happy to see that some training is currently being conducted for persons in cross-racial appointments, but we still have a long way to go.

6. *What personal gifts and graces have been assets to you during your years of ministry? Be specific and relate how they have been helpful.*

God has blessed me with many gifts and graces, but the ones I choose to highlight are as follows:

- It has been helpful to be a loving person and to extend that love to friends, enemies, and strangers. I know that love and forgiveness are two sides of the same coin, and I sought to express love in my relationships with all those entrusted to my care and to those whose paths crossed mine.
- The spirit of forgiveness has been most helpful to me personally. I have lived, taught, and emphasized forgiveness, so others could be open to a forgiving spirit. In my appointments where conflict occurred, I was intentional in praying for a forgiving spirit. God answered my prayers, and I was able to minister to those parishioners with a genuine caring spirit.
- I have learned that spiritual warfare is real, and I am able to keep in my heart that I am not fighting against the people, but against the spirits that are influencing and driving evil actions. Therefore, I am able to lovingly pray for those who misuse, abuse, and persecute me.
- I have the gifts of joy and encouragement, and they are contagious as well. I am able, with God's help, to lift people out of sadness and despair with words of encouragement and a joyful spirit. They become joyful themselves as a result of being in my presence. Being joyful is so critical as we witness about our Lord because people are encouraged when they see me joyful in my service to God.
- I know that God has called me to serve His people, to be an instrument of love, forgiveness, encouragement, and joy, and to be a vessel that can be used to build and further the kingdom of God. I take this call so seriously that I am able, with God's help, to be a blessing—even when it hurts.

7. List any particular accomplishments or honors conferred during your years of ministry.

- Annual Conference Preacher and Teacher in Western Pennsylvania, Michigan, and Wisconsin Annual Conferences.
- Conference Preacher for the Aldersgate National Conference on Spirit-Filled Living in Kentucky.
- Faculty of the Academy of Spiritual Formation of the UMC in Alabama.
- Workshop and retreat leader in Pennsylvania, Alabama, California, Wisconsin, Iowa, Virginia, West Virginia, Michigan, Ohio, and North Carolina.
- Founder and CEO of four nonprofit corporations in Pennsylvania.
- Director and associate dean of doctoral studies at United Theological Seminary in Dayton, Ohio.
- Church consultant and director of outreach missions in Western Pennsylvania Annual Conference.
- Presenter of a position paper at the combined national meeting of the American Academy of Religion and Society of Biblical Literature.
- Distinguished Alumnus Award of Pittsburgh Theological Seminary, Pittsburgh, Pennsylvania.
- Distinguished Alumnus Award of Methodist Theological Seminary in Delaware, Ohio.
- PhD in formative spirituality at Duquesne University, Pittsburgh, Pennsylvania.
- Liturgical dancer at the consecration services of two UMC bishops in Pennsylvania and Michigan.
- Liturgical dancer and choreographer of a dance troupe at twenty-fifth anniversary of the Institute of Formative Spirituality, Pittsburgh, Pennsylvania.
- Mayor's Pride Award: Outstanding Citizen of the Year, Washington, Pennsylvania.
- President of the Council of Churches in Troy, Ohio.
- President of the Black Seminarians organization at Pittsburgh Theological Seminary in Pittsburgh, Pennsylvania, and at MTSO in Delaware, Ohio.

CHAPTER THREE

Rev Dr. Tara Renee Sutton

Church: Halsey and Southmont
United Methodist Churches
City: Grand Blanc, Michigan
Conference: Detroit
Age: 53
Year accepted the call to ordained
ministry: June 17, 1985 (Father's Day)
Year Ordained: 1989 AME Church
Year accepted as full member in UMC: 1998

PHASE 1

1. *Recall significant events in your life and society, by decades, beginning with year 1–10, 10–20, etc., until the year you accepted the call to ordained ministry, even if your earlier years were not in a Christian setting. List any songs that were formative in the life events you include in your stories.*

YEARS 1–10

A significant event happened early in my life that I didn't find out until I was well into my late forties. My father told me that when I was a baby, he took me, held me in his hands, raised me up to heaven, and told the Lord that he was dedicating me back to Him. He was giving me back to God like in *Roots* where the father takes the child and raises him to heaven. As I reflect and analyze my life, as well as reviewing an internal assessment of my call, I can understand why I have such a strong relationship with God, even to this day.

I remember riding with relatives from Chicago to Detroit, and I was left in the car while my aunt ran into the bank. Suddenly, I had to go to the restroom. I went into the bank, where she was, but I couldn't find her. I didn't return to the car, but I started walking down the street. I didn't know exactly where I was going. It was an amazing situation because a police car picked me up and took me directly to the house where I was staying in Detroit. When I think about that whole situation, I still reflect on God's "hedge of protection" that he built around me. The policeman, I'm going to call him "Officer Friendly," was so kind. He took me to the right home, and I'm still grateful for that moment.

In my earlier years, when I was in the fifth or sixth grade, my mom started taking me over to my cousin's house, which was my father's brother and sister-in-law, and I would stay there during the summers. It was really a time of spiritual growth and awakening in my life. My aunt taught me my very first prayer. We knelt beside the bed and prayed, "Now I lay me down to sleep." That was the first prayer I learned, coupled with the importance of kneeling before God. That was a time of learning a spiritual discipline that I still observe and appreciate because it represents humility.

My aunt and uncle would go to the Baptist church, located in the South Side of Chicago, and they took my cousins and me to church. They taught us how to give money because my uncle would put a quarter and a dime on our table every Sunday. The dime was for one offering, and the quarter was for another one. They taught us the value of giving to God, and as I continued to progress in my relationship with Jesus Christ, I began to tithe. We also went to vacation Bible school. My two cousins and I would take the bus to VBS. The formation of my spiritual life really came from my aunt and uncle and how they really taught me about God. We didn't necessarily open the Bible throughout the week, but we listened to my aunt sing Christian songs in the home, and my uncle, the deacon in the church, was very committed to the Lord. Those were some significant times in reference to my relationship with the Lord.

I remember going to the corner store with my cousins, and we were trying to cross the street, but the traffic was a little heavy. They were holding my hand, but eventually I let go of their hand. I walked right into the middle of the street, and a car missed me by just a hair. God's hedge of protection was constantly around me.

I also went to spend a summer with my grandmother. I got out of the bunk bed to go to the bathroom, climbed back up to the top bunk, and went back to sleep. I woke up on the floor. I had fallen to the floor, but I was not hurt at all.

My cousin said, "What are you doing down here?"

I didn't have an answer. I think that was God's protection because if you fall off the top bunk, you usually injure yourself. However, I was not harmed or bruised. I did not attribute that to God then, but now that I reflect back on the fact that my father gave me back to God, I can see God's continual protection throughout my life.

YEARS 11–20

At the age of eleven, on a Sunday morning at the missionary Baptist church, when they opened the doors of the church, my cousins and I walked down and received the right hand of fellowship. Later on, we were baptized (fully immersed). My family members came on the day I was baptized, and we really enjoyed that time of celebration.

I continued to go to church with my aunt and uncle and my cousins, and we would sit maybe eight rows from the back. A lot of times, when the sermon was being preached, my cousins and I would sit there and write notes back to each other, not really paying attention to the sermon. One day, all three of us left the church and got into my aunt and uncle's car.

My uncle turned around and asked, "What was the sermon about today?"

None of us could respond because we weren't paying attention. As I continued to analyze and reflect deeply about what exactly was happening, it was almost like God turned around and said, "What did the pastor preach today?" It was a wake-up call in our lives. After that time, we would use the bulletin to take sermon notes. Of course, we would still pass other notes back and forth, like kids used to do anyway, but at least the sermon would get our attention. That was a big turning point for me.

I graduated as valedictorian from my high school in Chicago. The significance from that age, eleven to twenty, was experiencing the love of Jesus Christ through simple conversations, simple discussions, and simple dialogues. I hadn't necessarily tried to read the Bible at that time, but I surely was committed to going to church and being in conversation with the Lord. I would say God definitely guided my footsteps. I was preparing to go to college, and I prayed about which college I should attend, so I really connected with the Lord.

YEARS 20–30

When I went to college, I went astray. I did not attend church a lot once I got there. I went to the Baptist church in Evanston, Illinois, and was under watch care. I did attend on several occasions—but not consistently. I pledged a wonderful sorority, Alpha Kappa Alpha, and I was more attentive to pledging than to attending church. However, I continued to have conversations with God.

I distinctly remember having a conversation with God in December 1984. I heard God speaking to me. I was pondering my career in my dorm room because I had plans to be an attorney.

The voice of God said, "Why do you want to become an attorney?"

I said, "To make money."

Some other careers popped into my head—teacher, social worker, and preacher—and I said, "Ooh, I don't know if I want to be a preacher." I know that conversation didn't come from me directly. Surely God was having a conversation with me about my accepting my call into the ministry. However, I decided to start going to my father's church on the South Side of Chicago. From Evanston to the South Side of Chicago, on the bus and the train, it took an hour and a half one way, but I got on that train and bus, and I started going to my father's church. The church was St. James AME Church.

I became more active in the university chapel at Northwestern University. I was a liturgist and served there. In the winter of 1985, I went on a spiritual retreat that the Northwestern chapel provided. I really believe that God was beginning to reel me in closer to Him because He did have a calling on my life to preach. I went on the retreat to hear the voice of God and to begin to delve deeper into many conversations with the Lord.

I went home after my junior year, and on June 17, 1985, I woke up and decided to go to church. It was Father's Day. I went to St. James AME and sat in about the fourth row in front of the pulpit. When the preacher was preaching, I heard God so audibly that I had to turn around to see if someone was behind me.

God said, "I'm calling you into the ministry."

It really was God talking to me, and on that day, I joined the church.

The pastor was not there on that Sunday, so I set up an appointment with him for a week later. When I went into his office, before I could even take a seat, he said, "You've been called to the ministry."

The pastor didn't really know me, so I have concluded that God wanted to make sure I knew that He had called me. That started my journey into the ministry.

List any songs that were formative in the life events you include in your stories.

There were some songs that were formative in my life. I woke up many mornings with this song on my heart, "I Woke Up This Morning with My Mind Stayed on Jesus." When I first accepted the call to the ministry, I found a Gideon Bible at my mother's house, and every morning, I got up, read the Bible, and sang, "You Can't Make Me Doubt Him." Those two songs really helped deepen my faith in my formative years.

2. *Recall the people who significantly contributed to your Christian formation up to the acceptance of the call. Tell the stories of how they influenced your life.*

The first person who contributed to my Christian formation was my dad. He offered me back to God as an infant, and later, he was very supportive of me in ministry.

My aunt and uncle taught me a lot about the Christian life, and they took me to church every time I went to their home.

One of my college friends gave me sound spiritual advice when I became frustrated with my circumstances. I had been named "Sorer of the Year" and was soon to become chaplain of the sorority. I had been serving and giving my all to the sorority, yet I was internally frustrated. One day, when I was very sad, I was sharing my heart with her, and she told me to try Jesus. That was a moment of reawakening to the pitfalls of living my life for the sake of the world. It also shed a deeper light on the scripture that tells us we cannot serve God and mammon. I was doing many things that didn't represent Jesus Christ, and I had lost the joy of the Lord until she told me to try Jesus.

My mother was influential in my spiritual formation because she allowed me to go to my aunt's house where she knew I was being spiritually fed. Mother may not have known she was being used by God, but surely God used my aunt and uncle to open doors to his presence.

3. *Recall the people/events that significantly served to deter your affirming the call to ordained ministry.*

Once I accepted the call, both my father and mother were concerned. I can't say they deterred me, but they were concerned that I wouldn't be able to put food on my table.

In terms of a determent, I remember going into the Board of Ordained Ministry, and one examiner kept asking me questions that demonstrated he doubted my call. I finally said to him, "It is by faith that I believe God is calling me." That was not a deterrent, but a discouragement. No one deterred me from affirming my call.

4. When you received the call to ordained ministry, did you respond yes immediately and take appropriate action? Why or why not?

When I received the call on Father's Day, I took immediate action by scheduling an appointment with the pastor to pursue that call. I have never looked back on my calling to the ministry. I responded immediately, but I was delayed for a week because the pastor was not available immediately. Upon meeting with the pastor, he provided guidance for entering the ordained ministry.

5. What was your occupation when you received the call, and what effect did it have on your response?

I had just completed my junior year in college. I took immediate action and applied to Garrett Evangelical Theological Seminary after I accepted the call to ministry on June 17, 1985. I truly know that my trust and faith in God were sincere and had grown over the years— even though I had moments where I did go astray. I accepted my call immediately because I said to God, "Lord, if I died today, I would not be able to give you a reason why I said no." I immediately said yes. Six days after I applied to Garrett, my letter of acceptance was in the mail. God was confirming the call through the seminary.

6. If you did not take immediate action to the call, recall the thinking/ rationale that caused resistance to your immediate response.

I took immediate action.

7. What occurred that enabled you to overcome the resistance to answering the call?

I didn't resist the call, but I did need greater clarity. At first, I did not want to be a pastor, and I really struggled in terms of which direction God was leading me. When I was in seminary, I went into some in-depth prayer and decided to go to the Air Force in preparation to be a full-time chaplain. I went on three tours of duty: Montgomery, Alabama; Denver, Colorado; and Springfield, Illinois. After prayer and consultation with the Lord, I really didn't feel that that was the permanent direction I was to follow.

I started to work for MCI, a telephone company, when I first graduated from seminary. I left MCI and went to work for Urban Ministries, which publishes African American Sunday school and other curricula. I was also serving as a professor for Payne Theological Seminary and as co-pastor for seven years at Holy Trinity AME Church in Dolton, Illinois. While serving in these multiple capacities, I really desired to pastor my own congregation. My struggle was not in answering the call but in having a certainty of what the call was, even though the initial word from God was to preach. I struggled with myself.

8. What was the time frame between receiving the call and saying yes with appropriate action?

My timing was immediate. I responded immediately, but I was delayed for a week because the pastor was not available immediately.

9. What role did the church play in your answering or not answering the call immediately?

My church was very supportive, and they received me very well. The pastor of the church had previously been a presiding elder. The presiding elder is like a district superintendent in the United

Methodist Church, so he was able to walk me through the whole process of answering the call in St. James AME Church. The pastor allowed me to preach on Sunday mornings, and I preached a funeral as well. Every Sunday, I sat in the pulpit with the others who were pursuing ministry. We all participated by carrying out different responsibilities in the worship service. The church was a very good training ground. Several people accepted their call into ministry under the same pastor's administration.

10. *Were there any spiritual disciplines that played a role in your resistance or acceptance of the call? Tell the stories.*

I utilized several different spiritual disciplines. One discipline was Bible study that began as a child. Another discipline was prayer, and the other was worship. As I began to study the Bible, I fell in love with the Word of God, and I am still in love with the Word of God. Every time I open the Word, it reveals something different and gives me aha moments.

My prayer life has been an ongoing process of learning how to pray "unceasingly." This process began when I was younger, and I still have that same prayer conversation. I still talk to God out loud, and people say, "Who you talking to?" I still say, "I'm talking to God." I've learned to be in constant communication with the Lord—even for the simple things, like asking the Lord to help me find a parking space or asking Him where I should go to eat. I received the gift of speaking in tongues in college, and I still utilize that prayer language during my individual time as I seek God, listen to Him, and communicate intimately with Him.

The other discipline is worship. Worship is vital in my life. I do not just worship on Sundays; I worship every day in what I do and in what I don't do. I worship God in faithful obedience as a part of my everyday life.

11. *In retrospect, how do you see God's hand at work in your life that prepared you for ordained ministry?*

I gave some examples of God's hand at work in my life in previous questions, but I also believe I felt God's heart for people who have a relationship with him. I listened to the heartbeat of God, and I have really seen God moving in miraculous ways through prayer. As a result of my prayer life, I have become a prayer warrior. Through prayer, God has taught me that He doesn't give us what we can handle, but He helps us handle what we are given.

12. When you accepted the call to ministry, what was the response from persons in your life?

My mother really wanted me to go to law school, so initially, my being in ministry was not really her desire. She did not try to discourage me, but she did express her concern regarding my financial well-being. Over the years, she has grown in her relationship with God, and now she is happy that I am a pastor.

My father was definitely supportive, but he also was concerned about my financial status because he knew that most Black pastors in the AME church where I started didn't make a lot of money.

My husband, now my ex-husband, was not thrilled and had concerns.

My family members were very supportive. Nearly a hundred family members and friends came when I had my trial sermon.

My pastor was really encouraging and supportive. He mentored me and allowed me to perform pastoral duties from the beginning. Later, I was asked by a friend at Garrett to help co-pastor a congregation. We became co-pastors at Holy Trinity AME Church, and we really worked very well together.

PHASE 2

1.Tell the story of your first three years while meeting the requirements necessary for elder's or deacon's ordination or for local pastor's requirements. What were some of your struggles and victories as you pursued answering the call?

- *Share your stories with the Board(s) of Ordained Ministry. In what ways were they helpful? Did you have any identifiable issues that you were told to improve upon?*
- *If you were assigned to a church(s) during those first three years, what relationships did you have with the parishioners and the community?*
- *When you attended seminary or licensing school, what were your experiences with faculty, staff, and peers? Include the specific years?*

I started in the AME church in the Chicago Conference. I completed the deacon's track and then the elder's track two years later. The Board of Examiners in the AME church had required assignments. Since I was in the seminary, I was excused from some of those requirements. The Board of Examiners moved me forward on the ordained elder's track.

When I applied to Garrett Evangelical Seminary, I was accepted in six days, but I did not receive a scholarship until my second year. It was a good school, and I was blessed to be exposed to different denominations. Garrett was the only seminary I applied to. I was accepted.

I decided to transfer to the United Methodist Church. I received a letter from the Board of Ordained Ministry on January 1, 1998, that I had been accepted as a full member of the UM Church, but later I was informed that I needed to take UM history and polity. I also had to rewrite some papers. After fulfilling those additional requirements, I went before the board again and was received as a full elder. The identifiable issue that was pointed out was my need to relax and have fun. I was a workaholic.

Incidentally, I am finally getting close to enjoying my life while in ministry. I know there has to be balance. God does not require us to work until we get sick, but I still struggle with balance.

During my seminary days, I remained at St. James AME Church while being trained to be a pastor.

I was able to minister to my mom on some of the days when I

was able to go home. She joined me in church on a Sunday when I was home and had a highly inspirational encounter with Christ. God answered the prayer I had offered up for many years.

I attended seminary from 1986 until 1989. My seminary experiences were awesome, and I learned the discipline of writing sermons and other academic subjects on a weekly basis. One professor in particular strongly invited women to enter into ministry, and she used books and other resources by Georgia Harkness and women theologians. One of the systematic theologians discussed James Cone and others, making a large impact in my theology. Another professor was very charismatic and taught about laying on of hands, speaking in tongues, and being joyful. The varied approaches gave a holistic perspective to seminary academics, which made learning enjoyable as well as challenging.

I was fortunate to have two mentors in the AME church who greatly assisted in guiding and directing me along the way.

There was a wonderful woman in student services who was so helpful in housing and helping us integrate the various aspects of seminary life as Black students. She had great insight and wisdom.

In 1987, my second year of seminary, I began to commute. On one particular day, I was driving and got extremely sleepy and dozed off several times. Thank goodness God prevented an accident. I know God put a hedge of protection around me. On that day, I came to a deeper understanding of guardian angels.

2. *Share your stories of each individual appointment since beginning the process for ordination until 2016. Include the following:*

- *What lessons did you learn from each appointment?*
- *What meaningful relationships were established? Include personal, professional, and church member relationships.*
- *What was your personal and church financial state?*
- *Relate any successes or challenges you faced in each appointment. Were there any personal events that affected your ministry (weddings, deaths, or illnesses?)*

- *What Methodist, national, local, or world events affected your appointments? Explain how.*
- *Have any of the meaningful relationships established with your parishioners been continued over the years?*

FIRST APPOINTMENT:
ASSOCIATE PASTOR AT HOLY TRINITY AME IN DOLTON, ILLINOIS

I served with the senior pastor. It was a small new church start in a shared facility, and I was taught the importance of teamwork. I also learned that everyone will not accept you—even if you preach excellent sermons. Also, I received an invitation to become an adjunct professor at Payne Theological Seminary via satellite in a Chicago church.

Church member relationships were cordial, and I developed a loving and caring friendship with the pastor's sister and her children.

I got married while serving at Holy Trinity, and the congregation and staff were very supportive.

The new church started with ten members.

The church paid me a small salary. I also worked at the Urban Ministry Publishing Co., and that salary was adequate income for my needs. I learned how to hold two jobs and be active on the conference level.

I later moved out of state and began to serve in a United Methodist church.

SECOND APPOINTMENT:
PASTOR AT OAK PARK UNITED METHODIST CHURCH, 1998–2002

I was the first African American to serve, but I was not the first woman. They were in a bad financial state before I arrived.

I learned that if the church doesn't desire to grow and embrace the community, it will struggle. Some of the people had different views on ministry and theology. I learned I had to be faithful to the Word of God as I understood it.

While I was there, we had neighborhood tutoring and ministered to high school students. I told stories that gave them exposure to cultural activities and other inner-city ministries. Even when you do your best, including conducting door-to-door evangelism, you can tell when the season is over. I also started a second service to reach out, but it was not enough.

Some success occurred in the congregation, as they began to nurture each other, but few were willing to reach out to the community.

I participated in ecumenical services with other churches and developed a lasting relationship with a clergywoman in the CME church.

Oak Park United Methodist Church closed under my administration.

THIRD APPOINTMENT:
2001–2005, INTERIM ASSOCIATE PASTOR
AT WATERFORD CENTRAL UMC

I appreciated serving under the senior pastor. He was straightforward. He said what he meant and meant what he said. It was a large membership church of more than eight hundred members with a good staff. I got along well with the pastor, staff, and congregation. Occasionally, I experienced racism in the congregation, but I learned to rise above it and remember I was still called to follow God.

There were many excellent ministries that were involved in revival. Also, I was involved in Habitat for Humanity, and a house was built. In addition, I went on a mission trip to Mexico.

The church finances were excellent. It was a spotlight church because it conducted a capital campaign and paid off its debt. I was still married, and my personal finances were okay.

On a personal level, my mother got married in 2003, and I was part of her wedding. That was a most joyous time.

The senior pastor and some of the members became friends, and we remain in contact with each other.

I received my doctorate degree, and people from Waterford came to support me. Also, I was elected as a General and Jurisdictional Conference delegate. It was a joy.

FOURTH APPOINTMENT:
2005–2012, PASTOR OF BETHEL UNITED METHODIST CHURCH

This was an African American Church, and I was the first woman pastor. I loved the parishioners, but I needed to set boundaries for my health. I needed to get the proper exercise and eat properly. Every church has their own DNA, and in every church, there will be some who accept you and some who reject you.

It was a successful ministry. The first year we had 110 people join, and thirty-eight were baptized. We saw people grow spiritually as well.

The finances were stable, and I enjoyed my time there.

I had to learn to set and keep boundaries. I got too busy to pray and seek the Lord, and every aspect of my life suffered. I got divorced and had to move on as a single parent.

On a national scale, President Obama was elected, and some members of the church took a bus to the inauguration. Sadly, I could not go because I had a funeral.

I developed friendships while I was there. I still walk with two people from Bethel, and I communicate with others by phone. I also have a prayer partner from within the conference who I still pray with today.

FIFTH APPOINTMENT:
2012–2016, DISTRICT SUPERINTENDENT IN
THE DETROIT ANNUAL CONFERENCE

This appointment was a turning point in my life. I continued as a workaholic, and I later got very sick. Other district superintendents and the bishop insisted that I take Sabbath rests, vacations, and even ordinary days off. I had to leave the cabinet earlier than planned. My son was in college, and I struggled financially.

Nationally, the Flint, Michigan, water crisis occurred, and our district was one of the first on the scene with water filters.

I developed good relationships with some district superintendents and agency personnel. I am still in contact with them, and they have been encouraging to me.

3. Do you see any of your life stories depicted in the lives of the saints in the Bible? Was it helpful to see yourself in scripture as you journeyed in your appointments?

I have felt like Esther who believed in the power of prayer and fasting, realizing God moves in miraculous ways as we practice this discipline. When I was appointed as district superintendent, I saw myself as being called by God "for such a time as this" as Esther.

When I became ill, I related to Job who lost everything. I lost my financial base, lost weight, and felt a loss in my spiritual life.

When I was young in ministry, I was similar to the prophet Jeremiah who was shunned because he spoke the truth.

4. If you were the first Black woman, or among the firsts, in any of your appointments, state those firsts, and tell the stories. What words of wisdom would you pass on to others who may become pioneers during their ministry?

I was the first African American woman in every appointment.

What words of wisdom would you pass on to others who may become pioneers during their ministry?

- Be yourself.
- Explore new ministries.
- Keep a journal.

- Keep in touch with other African American clergywomen for support—even if not in the United Methodist Church.
- Have someone to confess to—it will help you grow.
- Stay prayed up.
- Laugh at yourself.
- When you come across racism or sexism, remember that it is not about you! Your fight is against a spirit—not a person.
- Always walk in love.
- Maintain intimacy with Christ, which allows God's blessings to flow through more easily.
- Create a vision statement and purpose for the ministry.
- Make time for yourself.

5. *In hindsight, how could the annual conference and/or other UM personnel be more helpful when assigning Black clergywomen as firsts in a given area of ministry?*

- The conference should bring someone in to have conversation with members of the church.
- There can be workshops where people can openly share their feelings and concerns.

6. *What personal gifts and graces have been assets to you during your years of ministry? Be specific and relate how they have been helpful.*

- I believe in prayer, and I am a prayer warrior. I also encourage people to actively engage in prayer with each other as a congregation.
- I have been given a spirit of discernment, which has enabled my congregations and district to prepare strategic mission and vision statements along with specific plans to accomplish those goals.
- I am an encourager, and this attribute is particularly helpful when we are actively engaged in change.

- I am also a helper. I assist others in moving to the next level and getting involved in ministries with a call to excellence.
- I am a teacher. I particularly teach prayer, spiritual formation, and praying in the spirit. I teach Christian education through various workshops.

7. List any particular accomplishments or honors conferred during your years of ministry.

- May 2017: One of forty-five outstanding alumni at Garrett-Evangelical Theological Seminary.
- 2015: Recipient of the Congressional Award for Outstanding Community Service.
- 2012: Recipient of an award for "Unwavering Service, Dedication, and Commitment" at Bethel.
- 2008: Unity of the Spirit Award in Flint, Michigan.
- 1997: Soror of the Year Award.
- District superintendent in the Detroit Annual Conference.

CHAPTER FOUR

Bishop Tracy S. Malone

Resident Bishop
Ohio East Episcopal Area
City: North Canton, Ohio
Age: 49 years old
Year Accepted the Call to Ordained
Ministry: 1982 (Age 13)
Year Ordained: 1993

PHASE 1

1. *Recall significant events in your life and society, by decades, beginning with year 1–10, 10–20, etc., until the year you accepted the call to ordained ministry, even if your earlier years were not in a Christian setting. List any songs that were formative in the life events you include in your stories.*

YEARS 1–10

Both of my parents had health challenges since I was a very small girl. The significant event, for the most part, was having to assume a lot of responsibility. I was the third oldest child, but I was the oldest girl. A lot of the responsibilities of cooking and taking care of my three younger siblings fell on me to make life a little easier for my parents since they were struggling to work and deal with their health challenges.

With my parent's health challenges, I matured a little sooner than the average child because of the additional responsibilities I had to take on. I became a caretaker very early in my life, and I saw my family, really, as my ministry, if you will, now that I reflect on it. Yes, the most significant challenge (or event) in my life was my parents' health.

YEARS 10–20

I accepted the call to ministry when I was thirteen, and I was enrolled in the Lay Servants Academy even at that young age.

Between thirteen and twenty, I had significant family events that evolved around my two older brothers. It was during that period of time that my older brothers were having some of their own personal struggles. They both ended up leaving home, and that was a very difficult time for my family and me. It tore the fabric of our family, and that was challenging and difficult for me. During that time, I spent even more time in the church because it became almost like a safe haven for me—that's where I got my peace.

My two brothers were three years and one and a half years older than me. Since we were close in age, the disruption and difficult dynamics were painful. No matter what my parents did to try to help them, they continued in their wayward lifestyles.

My family and I received support, during all this turmoil, from the church.

List any songs that were formative in the life events in your stories.

One particular song that really shaped and formed me, particularly during that time, is "Blessed Assurance." The refrain, "This is my story, this is my song," really became a song of praise for me, and it would strengthen me when I was doing too much or bearing too much responsibility.

The other song was "He Touched Me." I resonated with the words. Those two songs encouraged me and strengthened me during those particular years of challenge.

2. Recall the people who significantly contributed to your Christian formation up to the acceptance of the call. Tell the stories of how they influenced your life.

Both of my parents played a very key role by being grounded in their faith and attending church. My dad was a United Methodist pastor, and my mom was an elementary school teacher and a nurse. Even though they had a lot of health challenges, they never complained. They just did what they had to do and stayed bathed in prayer. I watched how they lived and adjusted to life. They could have given up on life, but their faith in God sustained them. They truly shaped and formed me very early in my life to truly trust in God.

There was a particular member of the church who took me under her wings because she realized I had a lot of things going on with my family. Periodically, she would take me to get something to eat just to have conversation and check on me. She made sure I was OK, and she bought my first bicycle. I watched how she lived her faith and how attentive she was toward my family and our needs. She also really inspired my faith.

3. Recall the people/events that significantly served to deter your affirming the call to ordained ministry.

I don't know if I could say a determent, but I will say that my father had concerns. He had accepted his call to ministry as a second career, and he was going through his own process for ordained ministry when I answered my call at thirteen. Because of his witness of what women clergy experienced in ministry, he didn't discourage me, but he had some serious concerns and reservations for me even considering the ordained ministry. He wasn't quite sure how accepting the church would be toward my leadership as a woman. I am not sure if it was for my protection—or his lack of assurance in female pastoral leadership—but he related his reservations. However, he never got in my way. Nevertheless, for a little while, I began to question whether or not I was moving in the right direction.

4. *When you received the call to ordained ministry, did you respond yes immediately and take appropriate action? Why or why not?*

When I received my call to ministry, I was attending a youth ministerial institute. The Maceo D. Pembroke Institute had a "Call to Commitment," and I remember going forward. They had a conversation with us about ministry as a vocation. At that time, I wasn't sure how I would serve the church. I knew that I was called to ministry, but I wasn't clear at that young age if it would be as a preacher or a missionary. The people who were there that night took my hand and prayed over me, and they encouraged me to take the next step by letting my pastor know. My pastor was my father. Therefore, I shared with him and my mother. My mother encouraged my father to connect me with a female pastor who would be able to sit with me and help me discern my call.

My father put me in touch with a female pastor who became my mentor, and she began to shepherd me through the discernment process. She, my mother, and my father were instrumental in getting me enrolled in the Lay Servant Academy (formally called Lay Speakers Academy). The academy was mostly adults, and it was the only step available because I was too young to start the process for ordained ministry. I completed the academy, and even as a teenager, I started preaching "Youth Sundays." People would invite me to preach, and my clergywoman mentor was the very first person who invited me to preach at her church.

5. *What was your occupation when you received the call, and what effect did it have on your response?*

I was a student, and the call to ministry made me feel a little awkward around my friends. It wasn't popular for me to say I wanted to be a minister or a pastor when I grow up. When I shared my vocational goals, I was treated a little differently. When my peers would have different parties and other things they were doing, I wasn't invited because of their perception of what a pastor is or ought to be and do. They assumed I would not come or would not want to be a part of it because of what I said I wanted to be. The call did have a negative impact on my life. I learned very early how you can be isolated and/or treated differently when you aspire to be a pastor. However, I was not apologetic. Even in my high school yearbook, where it says ambition, I indicated minister, so I became bold in my call.

6. *If you did not take immediate action to the call, recall the thinking/ rationale that caused resistance to your immediate response.*

In my case, it was an immediate response. When I felt the call at the youth institute when I was thirteen, my immediate response was to go to my pastor—my father—and I immediately responded to the call. Of course, because of my age, I couldn't start the candidacy process, but I was enrolled in the Lay Servants Academy.

What was the time frame between receiving the call and taking appropriate action?

Receiving the call, having that definite yes, and knowing this was what I was supposed to be doing came in my college years. I was involved in campus ministry, and I had an internship through the General Board of Global Ministries. My call became clearer during those intern years. It would have been my junior year of college in 1989. I would have been about twenty years of age.

7. *What occurred that enabled you to overcome the resistance to answering the call?*

When the internship occurred, I was placed in Columbus, Georgia, for an entire summer. I was living with a family I did not know and working at a community house for abused women. I had the opportunity to be present with those women by leading some Bible studies and being responsible for the weekly devotions. I saw how my leadership and presence with those hurting and broken women was really making a difference. I was bringing them comfort and affecting their lives, but my life was also being shaped. My faith was being shaped by being in ministry and in a relationship with them. My questions about my call became a "Yes, this is what I am supposed to be doing." It felt right, and it felt comfortable. I was not just a caretaker and supervisor of the community house, but my ministry was really being formed. It felt like I was on the right track.

8. *What was the time frame between receiving the call and saying yes with appropriate action?*

I took the appropriate action at age thirteen.

9. *What role did the church play in your answering or not answering the call immediately?*

An incredibly supportive role came from the church where I grew up. First, I was given the opportunity to attend that Pembroke Institute, the place where I accepted my call. It was the church that saw the gifts in me that sent me there. I had to have signatures and recommendation letters, so I believe that they saw something in me.

Then, of course, accepting my call and completing the Lay Servants Institute was another significant supportive role. Not many thirteen-year-olds attend that institute. Churches started inviting me to preach while I was in high school. Again, that was support, affirmation, encouragement, and nurture from local churches. I can only imagine that my messages weren't as strong as they could have been—being a teenager—but they encouraged me and nurtured me along. I just kept keeping on!

The church has always played a significant role in the nurturing and the formation of my call.

10. *Were there any spiritual disciplines that played a role in your resistance or acceptance of the call? Tell the stories.*

Again, mine would be more acceptance of the call. Two particular spiritual disciplines were prayer and fasting. When I was doing my internship in Columbus, Georgia, I would pray very often and fast one day a week. I would intentionally fast because I was really in my discernment phase. I was trying to figure out what I was to do with this call. *Where am I supposed to go in life?* My college campus minister helped me get the internship and encouraged me to use it as a time to really discern my call.

Once a week, I would fast, and that would be a time for me to truly be before the Lord, seeking God's wisdom and directions. Prayer was an integral part from my young years up through my entire life. I always had the spiritual discipline of an intentional prayer life that has always formed my faith.

Prayer has always been a discipline for me, but fasting became a new spiritual discipline for me as I was doing the internship.

A third spiritual discipline that has made a significant difference in my life is studying the Word of God. Preparing for those Bible studies every week when I was an intern began a consistent journey of Bible study.

Last, but not least, was having to preach and being invited to preach. I started the preaching discipline when I was thirteen or fourteen, and it has continued to this day.

Part of my acceptance of the call was accepting those opportunities along with all the preparation and practice. Studying the Word of God, practicing prayer, fasting, and preaching really helped cement my call for me—and the acceptance of my call.

11. *In retrospect, how do you see God's hand at work in your life that prepared you for ordained ministry?*

I really think that what I just shared about going through my teenage years, and then, of course, graduating college. I went to seminary immediately after college. During my college years and my seminary years, the different opportunities I had to serve really helped to prepare me for ministry.

While in college, I was hired as a youth director at a local Methodist church. In seminary, my field education experiences were at St. Mark's United Methodist Church in Chicago.

My life journey has really helped prepare me for the ordained ministry. The internship, being hired by the local church, the field education experiences, college and seminary, Lay Servant Institute, and local church leadership all played significant roles.

Another significant factor in preparation for ministry was my parents' health, which continued to fail and progressively got worse. I graduated seminary in 1993 and was ordained and got married in 1993. In 1995, when I was serving in my first appointment as an associate pastor, my mother died. Eight months later, in May 1996, my father died. I was involved in their care from college until the time of their death. In retrospect, I see my caring for them, while still pursuing my call—meeting the requirements of college and seminary and then pastoring—were also part of my preparation. My experiences prepared me to have empathy for other families serving as caretakers and even the pain of having lost my parents to death and having loved ones incarcerated. From joy to turmoil to death, all those experiences helped prepare me for ministry.

In retrospect, I think I am the pastor that I am, the leader that I am, and the bishop that I am because of being shaped by all those experiences. All of that was preparation.

12. *When you accepted the call to ministry, what was the response from persons in your life?*

I received overwhelming support from my mother and from the church. People were excited! Since I was a child of the church, people were excited.

My father had reservations, but as he watched me through my teenage years—preaching in different churches, going to college, doing the internship and serving—he was overjoyed and so proud of the person and pastor I was becoming. His initial reservations of his not knowing how the church would accept me and then seeing how the church was accepting me gave him more freedom to say, "OK, she's going to be all right!"

PHASE 2

1. *Tell the story of your first three years while meeting the requirements necessary for elder's or deacon's ordination or for local pastor's requirements. What were some of your struggles and victories as you pursued answering the call?*

- *Share your stories with the Board(s) of Ordained Ministry. In what ways were they helpful? Did you have any identifiable issues that you were told to improve upon?*
- *If you were assigned to a church(s) during those first three years, what relationships did you have with the parishioners and the community?*
- *When you attended seminary or licensing school, what were your experiences with faculty, staff, and peers? Include the specific years?*

I received the call to ministry at the age of thirteen, and even at that early age, I was trying to discern and determine if the call was to be an elder, a deacon, or a local pastor. My father and mother recognized the struggle and surrounded me with women to help me discern the call. By the time I pursued the formal elder process, I had a support system in place, which provided further opportunities to pursue and discern the call.

The Board of Ordained Ministry (BOOM) was very supportive. When I had my final interview, one of the members of the Board of Ordained Ministry interpreted my pursuit of the ministry as ambitious in a negative way. Unfortunately, that person didn't see that my passion and excitement was due to my long journey, which started at age thirteen, coming to fruition. That person suggested perhaps I needed to tone it down, but others believed my excitement was an expression of cultural differences. The board did not identify any issues to improve upon. They encouraged me to keep working on balance between married life, care of parents, and ministry responsibilities.

I attended Garrett Seminary from 1990 until 1993. I had very good faculty, staff, and peer relationships. I fully experienced communal life, and I was involved in the board of trustees as a student. Seminary life was very formational and helped me discern my call to ordained ministry as an elder.

2. Share your stories of each individual appointment since beginning the process for ordination until 2016. Include the following:

- *What lessons did you learn from each appointment?*
- *What meaningful relationships were established? Include personal, professional, and church member relationships.*
- *What was your personal and church financial state?*
- *Relate any successes or challenges you faced in each appointment. Were there any personal events that affected your ministry (weddings, deaths, or illnesses?)*
- *What Methodist, national, local, or world events affected your appointments. Explain how.*
- *Have any of the meaningful relationships established with your parishioners been continued over the years?*

FIRST APPOINTMENT:
1993–1996, FIRST UMC, LOMBARD

My first appointment was from 1993 until 1996 as associate pastor of First UMC, Lombard. It was a cross-racial appointment. My relationships with the parishioners were healthy and welcoming. The first couple of years were a little bumpy. Fortunately, we were able to work through the challenges.

SECOND APPOINTMENT:
1996–2001, PASTOR, SOUTHLAWN UMC

My second appointment was 1996–2001 at the Southlawn UMC, in the inner city of Chicago. Phenomenal ministry occurred there. The church was experiencing brokenness from a previous conflict when I arrived, and I focused on healing. I also needed healing because I lost my mother in 1995, and in 1996, my father died. Consequently, both the congregation and I grew healthy together. Good ministries were birthed, and some wonderful relationships were established. My first child was born during this ministry, and it had a very positive impact on the church. Personal friends at the church became the godparents, and those relationships remain strong.

The financial state of the church was healthy. My personal finances were also healthy.

As the church began to heal, we moved from primary emphasis on healing to discipleship. New families began joining and the church started to grow.

THIRD APPOINTMENT:
2001–2007, SENIOR PASTOR OF WESLEY UMC, AURORA, ILLINOIS

Wesley UMC, in Aurora, Illinois, was my third appointment. I was the first female senior pastor, the first ethnic senior pastor, and the first senior pastor under forty. We began to focus on teaching, developing emerging leadership, and building discipleship systems within. Those with previous issues with me began to embrace me, my family, and the ministries of the church.

We developed a culture that faced issues by naming them, holding people accountable, and developing plans to address the issues. In retrospect, I can see that there should have been some prework done by the cabinet. Nevertheless, we had success with the creation of new ministries and with multicultural activities. My second child was born, and it also had a positive impact on the church.

The tragedy of 9/11 was instrumental in bringing forth cooperation of Ecumenical leaders for prayer vigils and worship services. The leaders were also intentional in addressing fear in the dialogues, which also helped my congregation.

Some friendships and acquaintances are still maintained through Facebook and other social media.

Fourth Appointment:
2007–2011, pastor, Gary UMC, Wheaton, Illinois

From 2007 until 2011, I was appointed to Gary UMC, in Wheaton, Illinois, a larger cross-racial downtown church. I was the first female of color, and lessons I had previously learned were helpful. I requested prework before I started, and it was done. Church leadership and pastor relations got off to a good start. A few issues emerged, but the congregation fought those battles. That was a very positive way to address conflict.

Good relationships were established. Basically, the church was healthy, but it was struggling under a $4 million debt from building renovation. The mortgage was a heavy burden, and it required another major campaign. During my leadership, the church moved from a debt of $4 million to $1.3 million in three years. New leadership emerged, new ministries were initiated, and intentionality of developing more inclusive ministries led to increased growth and retiring of debt.

Obama was elected president, and there was a change in the congregation as it shifted to more openness to the president. That openness was directly connected to my leadership at the church level. Perspectives changed toward Black leadership. A recession also occurred in the country.

The different institutions in Wheaton asked me to give key leadership for a variety of events, including the MLK Jr. celebration. To God be the glory.

Many relationships remain from that appointment.

FIFTH APPOINTMENT:
2011–2016, DISTRICT SUPERINTENDENT, CHICAGO SOUTHERN REGION

I was appointed district superintendent of the Chicago Southern Region in 2011 and served until 2016.

I became more efficient in supervisory duties, conflict transformation, and equipping leaders. I became astutely aware that not all conflict can be resolved, and not all conflict is bad. Conflict can be transformative, giving birth to new life.

District finances were challenging as we struggled with churches paying their apportionments, and we struggled to find money for ministry in the inner city. Also, suburban churches were encouraged to see that their missional partnership could be leveraged for the benefit of the entire district. Simultaneously, there were new developing ministries, including new multicultural ministries.

There were no personal events except for my nomination as an episcopal candidate.

Many colleagues were my friends, and they respected my role. I was careful to differentiate between supervisor and friend. The laity knew I had clergy relationships, but that did not undermine how I handled issues. I sought to establish trust and utilize diplomacy as I handled concerns and issues.

SIXTH ASSIGNMENT:
2016, ELECTED BISHOP, EAST OHIO CONFERENCE

I was elected as bishop and was assigned to the East Ohio Conference.

3. *Do you see any of your life stories depicted in the lives of the saints in the Bible? Was it helpful to see yourself in scripture as you journeyed in your appointments?*

I see my life in Moses who had great responsibilities, far beyond what he could handle individually, so he heeded the wisdom of Jethro by designating others to assist. Utilizing this principle helped me develop better leadership in each local church as district superintendent and then as bishop.

I identify with Esther who was called "for such a time as this." Like with Esther, God calls and gives wisdom for wherever we are. We receive strength and courage for hard times and difficult places.

4. *If you were the first Black woman, or among the firsts, in any of your appointments, state those firsts, and tell the stories. What words of wisdom would you pass on to others who may become pioneers during their ministry?*

Being a pioneer has been weaved through my ministry appointments:

- First Black clergywoman at First UMC, Lombard, Illinois.
- First woman and Black clergywoman at Wesley UMC, Aurora, Illinois.
- First woman and first Black clergywoman at Gary UMC, Wheaton, Illinois.
- First Black female district superintendent of the Chicago Southern District.
- First woman and Black female bishop assigned to Ohio East Annual Conference.

What words of wisdom would you pass on to others who may become pioneers during their ministry?

- Being a first has a divine purpose for utilizing your leadership.
- See the various leadership positions as both a gift and a challenge.

- Be yourself.
- Give God your best, and your gift will make room for you.
- Be the best you can be.
- Work with what you have.

5. In hindsight, how could the annual conference and/or other UM personnel be more helpful when signing Black clergywomen as firsts in a given area of ministry?

Prior to the appointment, there should be specific preparation of church leadership and the Black clergywoman.

- Opportunities should be provided for open discussion in developing support for relationships and ministries, as well as plans for addressing issues. These preparatory actions would help facilitate getting off to a better start. Similar action occurred at Gary UMC, and it made a significant difference.
- The bishop and cabinet must not forget that steps to teach cultural competency and openness to receive people of color and women will help bridge the cultural, racial, and gender divide and lead to more fruitful ministries of the local church and conference.
- The conference should utilize tools and resources from the general commission on the status and role of women, while building support systems to be utilized. The bishop, cabinet, church family, clergywomen, and other persons in the connectional system are all accountable for healthy relationships.

6. What personal gifts and graces have been assets to you during your years of ministry? Be specific and relate how they have been helpful.

- I have learned all people relate better with people as they get to know them. I create space for that. I am intentional in building an authentic community, especially in conflict.

I care about people even when I am required to make hard decisions.

- Administratively, I am very organized. I see the big picture and utilize my visionary skills. I work diligently to put building blocks in place to give legs to our ideas.
- I don't have to be the center of all efforts. Therefore, I intentionally involve others.
- I am comfortable preaching in different ministry contexts.
- I have cultivated the ability to listen deeply. I lead by listening. I always ask, "Do you feel you have been heard?" I am intentional in giving the other person an opportunity to respond to that question. I facilitate and cultivate an atmosphere where others are validated, heard, and cared for.
- In reflection, my life has embodied a pioneering motif.

7. List any particular accomplishments or honors conferred during your years of ministry.

- 2012 Award as Distinguished Alum of North Central College.
- 2016 Distinguished Alum, Garrett Seminary.
- Chicago BMCR: First clergy recipient of the Leadership Excellence Award.
- National BMCR: Outstanding Leadership Achievement Award.
- Planting new ministries in the Northern Illinois Conference.
- First elected bishop in 2016.
- First Black female bishop to be elected from the Northern Illinois Conference.

I also reduced major renovation debt in three years at Gary UMC, and the church retired the debt one year after I left.

CHAPTER FIVE

Rev. Cheryl Jefferson Bell

Congregational Care Pastor
Church: United Methodist Church
of the Resurrection
City: Leawood, Kansas
Conference: Great Plains Conference
Age: 61
Year accepted call to ordained ministry: 1990
Year Ordained: 1995

PHASE 1

1. *Recall significant events in your life and society, by decades, beginning with year 1–10, 10–20, etc., until the year you accepted the call to ordained ministry, even if your earlier years were not in a Christian setting. List any songs that were formative in the life events you include in your stories.*

YEARS 1–10

I was born and raised in Detroit, Michigan. My parents divorced when I was three years old. My father had custody of my brother and me. I felt like my mother was taken from me. This has been a hole in my heart and soul that, even to this day, is tender. We ended up living with a cousin and her family. She was my cousin, and we called her aunt, but she was like my mother. I am fourth-generation Methodist. Our family stayed with the Methodist Episcopal Church when other Black members left and joined Black denominations to avoid racist practices. The women of our family are strong Wesleyan Society United Methodist Women.

YEARS 10–20

This was a turbulent and violent time in my life. For three years, from ten to twelve years of age, my brother and I lived in Atlanta, Georgia. We lived with my grandmother and her sister in the family home. This was a period when my father was saving up to get us a home back in Detroit. I was subjected to sexual abuse by a relative. There was great relief when we finally moved back to Detroit. I finished high school and went to Spelman College and Georgia Tech in Atlanta. As I pursued my higher education, I was successful in academia, but I was a wounded soul.

I attended church regularly through graduation from high school, being confirmed, and participating in choir and youth fellowship. My father made sure we attended church, but he didn't attend himself. We worshiped at Conant Avenue UMC, where my uncle was a member, and I experienced the Spirit of God when I was confirmed with the laying of hands by my pastor.

I believe the seed of my calling was planted in my home church. I discovered the gift of singing. Worship was my lifeline until I left for college. I didn't grace the door of a church while in college until I went home for breaks. Our family church was founded by my great-grandfather, but he had a stronger pull on me than church did during that time.

YEARS 20–30

I graduated from my colleges in 1979 and 1980. I was twenty-three. My first job was with Mobil Oil. I traveled around the world, worked in western Texas, and worked on a ship, which took me overseas. I married a couple of weeks before my twenty-eighth birthday. Before our first anniversary, we learned that our working arrangements—I was on land, and he was at sea—weren't working. He found another job with Boeing in Wichita, Kansas (he is an engineer as well). I was also hired. We moved to Wichita in 1985. I was twenty-nine. Our life was good. I found a church home and volunteered in church and the community.

YEARS 30–40

My husband and I became lay speakers through Saint Mark UMC in Wichita, Kansas. Our church went without a pastor for a few months. During that time, the lay leadership, in which both my husband and I were part, provided leadership for the congregation. That was an experience that I believe also nurtured my calling. By the time our new pastor came aboard, our congregation was ready. Our local church went from being a mission church to becoming the largest church in our conference. Being part of that movement fueled my desire to serve and provided the "fertilizer" to the calling God had upon my life!

2. *Recall the people who significantly contributed to your Christian formation up to the acceptance of the call. Tell the stories of how they influenced your life.*

My great-grandfather was a Methodist pastor. He was a "church starter" in Atlanta. Educated through the church, his devotion to the church was passed down through the generations. It was mainly the women in our family who responded to the call to serve in the church.

Since women were restricted from serving as pastors, the women in my family got involved as best they could by being musicians, participating in women's ministry, and teaching. My grandmother, her sister, and their daughters lived lives of faith that were examples for me.

My cousin was like a mother, and she instilled the love of the United Methodist Women in me. Her role in my life as a mother figure was a demonstration of the strength of women and her love of the UMC and UMW. She has always been encouraging to me.

My uncle whose church we attended when growing up (Conant Avenue UMC) and my uncle who is a USAF retiree, took my brother and me under their wings, helping us get acclimated to the church and cultivating our involvement in the ministries. A Tuskegee airman and POW, my uncle's strength and faithfulness have always been a model for me while growing up. He was so excited to hear of my calling. He often says, "Your grandmother would be so proud!"

The pastor and his wife at Hamilton Park UMC in Dallas, Texas, were instrumental in my reconnecting with Christ while I was working as an engineer. I worked unusual schedules: two weeks on and one week off and two months on and one month off. Our transition days were usually on Sundays. I would do everything I could to make it back to town for worship. I would drive across Texas late on Saturday nights and early on Sunday mornings to make it in time for church! My love and desire to worship and serve God were nurtured during this time. I'm thankful for the acceptance and support of the pastor and congregation during my five years in Dallas.

Moving to Wichita, Kansas in 1985 to work for Boeing, my engineering husband and I found ourselves in a new land. Wanting to stay connected with the UMC, I looked for a Black UMC. Being in Wichita, there was only one at the time. This was when I became part of the Saint Mark UMC in Wichita, Kansas. They welcomed me with open arms! I knew that I had found my spiritual home. I was blessed to find a church that reminded me of Hamilton Park and Conant Avenue, and I never left!

At first, it was the laity who nurtured me. They showed me what it means to be an empowered layperson in the UMC. I became a lay speaker and was part of the team that sustained our church when we were in between pastors. My confidence was nurtured and built up by this amazing congregation.

The new pastor was the one who first asked me about serving full-time as a pastor. He helped plant the seed, but another pastor encouraged and supported me during my "calling" days. I was the first of many who accepted their calls into ministry under this pastor's leadership.

3. Recall the people/events that significantly served to deter your affirming the call to ordained ministry.

I was really affirmed throughout my calling.

4. When you received the call to ordained ministry, did you respond yes immediately and take appropriate action? Why or why not?

When my pastor, in 1990, asked me if I had considered serving in the church full-time, I said, "I think I am ready." This was the second "ask" for me. The first time, in 1988, the seed was planted, but I wasn't ready yet! The second ask came under new pastoral leadership, and my involvement had increased in the life of the church. I was primed and ready. I said yes and proceeded to take the steps to begin the adventure! I quit my engineering job and enrolled in seminary. On top of that, my husband and I proceeded to become foster parents for our daughter's siblings. When they came to live with us, they were five weeks, fifteen months, and five years old. Our daughter was four years old. It was a crazy time, but God was with us through it all.

5. What was your occupation when you received the call, and what effect did it have on your response?

As an electrical engineer, I was working in systems engineering at Boeing in Wichita, Kansas. I had been an engineer for ten years when

I accepted my call. Besides "the money," I was doing well, progressing, and succeeding in my profession. However, I got to a place where I was receiving more satisfaction from my participation in church than I did at work. I was not being fulfilled at work. My experience was a good foundation for my eventual service in the church, and it is a good connection point with others when they learn of my prior profession.

6. If you did not take immediate action to the call, recall the thinking/ rationale that caused resistance to your immediate response.

When my pastor, in 1988, asked me if I had considered serving in the church full-time, I said "Oh, no. I'm making too much money. God surely wouldn't be calling me." Evidently, I was not ready! I had been married for four short years. We adopted our daughter in 1988, and my mother died in 1988. There was a lot going on in our lives. It wasn't the time, I thought, for making a big career change, but the seed was planted.

At that time, I started entertaining the idea of being a pastor and working in and for the church full-time. When the second call came in 1990, I was ready.

7. What occurred that enabled you to overcome the resistance to answering the call?

Going through the UMC's discernment process was very helpful. It helped me look within and touch base with family, friends, and colleagues. I really appreciated going through the process, being affirmed by everyone I talked to.

8. What was the time frame between receiving the call and saying yes with appropriate action?

I first received the call in 1988, but I did not say yes to the call until 1990. Once I said yes, after telling my husband at the time and then my pastor, I hit the ground running. My process was interesting and quick. I put in my notice of resignation from my engineering position, started the candidacy process, applied, and was accepted into the seminary. On the home front, we went from two full-time engineering salaries—and our family went from one to four children. All of this took place within a three-month period! God opened doors, and the adventure began!

9. What role did the church play in your answering or not answering the call immediately?

Saint Mark UMC played a critical role in me answering my call in 1990. The senior pastor was totally on board, and he led the way. I was incorporated into the pastoral leadership of the church, which provided opportunities to participate in worship and other ways in the life of the local church. The congregation reinforced and affirmed my calling while paying the respect that comes with the office. I was one of the members transitioning into a leadership role, and my church family was very supportive!

10. Were there any spiritual disciplines that played a role in your resistance or acceptance of the call? Tell the stories.

Worship and prayer have been the primary spiritual disciplines and practices that have sustained and nurtured my call. When I was living in Dallas, I remember how my thirst for God was nurtured through worship. I longed to make it back to church on Sunday mornings, even if it meant that I had to drive all night to make it there. My pastor remarked how I would strive to make it to church each weekend that I could. Worship has been and continues to be my lifeline, my way of staying connected to God, and keeping me sane in an insane world. Prayer, unceasing prayer, as described by Brother Lawrence as experiencing the presence of God, has been the way that I have survived life!

I worked on a boat for a little more than two years, and in the middle of the water, surrounded by 360 degrees of water, I had a "coming to Jesus" moment. I was sitting on the deck at night. The moon was full and casting shadows. It was not a common experience, coming from Detroit, and I was reminded of Psalm 139. I realized there was nowhere I could go from the presence of God. This experience was a pivotal point on my spiritual journey—a seed planted that helped the call to be nurtured in my soul!

11. *In retrospect, how do you see God's hand at work in your life that prepared you for ordained ministry?*

I believe that my life's journey—the ups and downs, the joys and disappointments, the abuses and nurturing—have prepared me for doing ministry, grounded in a deep love and appreciation for God and God's people. My experiences—in my career, in life, and in the church—have provided me with an empathetic spirit that helps me minister and love others as God has loved me. From my family heritage, throughout my life's journey, to this moment, I see over, and over, and over again that I was called to serve God through the church!

12. *When you accepted the call to ministry, what was the response from persons in your life?*

There was excitement and support from family and friends—and even my husband (at the time). Their affirmation of my calling was a confirmation to me that I did make the correct discernment and decision to make this amazing career change and serve God in this amazing way.

PHASE 2

1. *Tell the story of your first three years while meeting the requirements necessary for elder's or deacon's ordination or for local pastor's requirements. What were some of your struggles and victories as you pursued answering the call?*

- *Share your stories with the Board(s) of Ordained Ministry. In what ways were they helpful? Did you have any identifiable issues that you were told to improve upon?*
- *If you were assigned to a church(s) during those first three years, what relationships did you have with the parishioners and the community?*
- *When you attended seminary or licensing school, what were your experiences with faculty, staff, and peers? Include the specific years.*

I entered the process when we were ordained twice: once as deacon and then as elder. I was ordained deacon in 1992 and elder in 1995. I graduated from Phillips Graduate Seminary in Enid, Oklahoma (known now as Phillips Theological Seminary in Tulsa, Oklahoma) in 1993.

My whole process, from my local church with the district and conference Boards of Ordained Ministry, was a blessing! I was approved without any known hesitation from the boards. I was nervous, of course, but the process was affirming and supportive of my call.

I worked part-time on the staff at my home church, Saint Mark UMC, in Wichita, Kansas, when I first began seminary in 1990. However, I quickly learned that I couldn't do seminary, help raise four children, and work all at once! In 1991, I let go of my position at the church and focused on school and family!

I was able to be appointed as an associate pastor at Saint Mark on July 1, 1993, which was following my graduation with my MDiv. That appointment lasted until I was appointed the pastor of a two-point charge in August 1995.

2. Share your stories of each individual appointment since beginning the process for ordination until year 2016. Include the following:

- *What lessons did you learn from each appointment?*
- *What meaningful relationships were established? Include personal, professional, and church member relationships.*

- *What was your personal and church financial state?*
- *Relate any successes or challenges you faced in each appointment. Were there any personal events that affected your ministry (weddings, deaths, illness, etc.)?*
- *What Methodist, national, local, or world events affected national, local, or world events affected your appointments? Explain how.*
- *Have any of the meaningful relationships established with your parishioners been continued over the years?*

First Appointment:
1993–1995, associate pastor of Saint Mark UMC, Wichita, Kansas

My first appointment was following my graduation with my MDiv in 1993. That appointment lasted until I was appointed the pastor of a two-point charge in 1995. Saint Mark is my church home, and that appointment was special compared to others I have held. I was the first female appointed there—as well as the first full-time associate pastor. It was hard but meaningful work. The people there are family to me, being the church we chose upon moving to the area. I looked for a Black United Methodist church in Wichita, and in 1985, it was the only one! I was greeted and welcomed just like family.

Our church was continuing to grow under the leadership of the senior pastor. As a staff, we learned how to be flexible, movable, and agile in our ministry. The growth kept us on our toes.

There were, however, challenges because it was my home church. Setting boundaries has always been a challenge for me, and it remained so when it came to my church family. It was extra difficult for me to draw lines with family. However, the relationships established during that time will be for a lifetime! It was the place I was nurtured in the faith and where I accepted my call to full-time ministry and the church that set me on a good path of ministry!

One thing, as I look back, began with my leaving Saint Mark. We were in the process of finishing up a capital campaign, and my family and I participated in that fully, from day one. However, when I received an off-appointment year assignment, I missed out on the occupation of that new space. It seemed that was just the beginning of such timing in my appointive career. I have been back to worship there, but I do miss not being able to have enjoyed that first Sunday in the new space.

SECOND APPOINTMENT:
1995–1999, PASTOR OF PRETTY PRAIRIE AND MURDOCK UMC, PRETTY PRAIRIE AND MURDOCK, KANSAS

This turned out to be one of my most important and life-changing appointments. It was a cross-racial and cross-cultural appointment with an African American female pastor from Wichita, Kansas, who grew up in Detroit, Michigan, who was appointed to two White rural churches. The largest church was in a town of 650 people, and the other was in an unincorporated town, where the post office and church were the main institutions in town! Our family integrated the town of Pretty Prairie, adding four African American children. There was also a mixed-race couple who were part of the community when we moved there. I followed the first female pastor for that charge!

I learned about farming, combines, making sausage, not praying for "no rain," rural America, the benefits and blessings of small towns, and the goodness of God's people.

We did great ministry together. We received an award for growth for rural congregations. They responded to my leadership, and I responded to their care, love, dedication, and openness. In the beginning, I told both congregations that I believed that God had brought us together for such a time as this. I wouldn't expect them to be like me, and I hoped they wouldn't expect me to be like them. What we would be together would be a blessing for all. And it was.

When I first arrived, with my children, who were five, six, nine, and ten, and without my husband, who was working in Wichita, this congregation took amazing care of me and my children. I didn't have to worry about trying to keep up with them while trying to unpack and get started with my ministry. That type of care and support was strong for my entire appointment!

One story I must share is that our United Methodist church, together with the Mennonite church and community of Pretty Prairie, were able to save our local care home. It was a battle, but we did it. The turning point was during a community meeting—when the owners of the care home informed us of actions that were to take place without the input or consultation of the community.

They were going to close it down. The Mennonite church didn't have a pastor at the time. They needed someone to speak up, and the Spirit of God prompted me to speak. That was all that it took for others to join in. Together, as the community, we were able to reopen the care home and bring it under the ownership of the community. It continues to this day as a viable and thriving care home for the community. I've been asked to come back to celebrate anniversaries. It was a great achievement for us all!

THIRD APPOINTMENT:
1999–2001, EXECUTIVE DIRECTOR OF UNITED
METHODIST URBAN MINISTRY (NOW UNITED
METHODIST OPEN DOOR), WICHITA, KANSAS

This extension ministry position satisfied two desires of my heart: moving back to the Wichita area, where my husband worked, and doing hands-on ministry to help those in need within our community. I came to this social service ministry from a successful appointment. It was an organization that had been under the leadership of a long-term executive minister. I was their first female executive director. A woman followed me and continues to this day, doing an amazing job!

There were difficult times with a sister organization, and there were changes that had to be made. It was a fulfilling ministry, as far as the outreach was concerned. We developed fundraising and connections with the community and helped incorporate structural changes. The boards of directors were amazing and supportive. It was during a season of change that I was brought on. I hope and pray that my short stint helped the organization become the great organization that it is today.

FOURTH, FIFTH, AND SIXTH APPOINTMENTS:
DISTRICT SUPERINTENDENT OF SALINA DISTRICT, 2001–2002; DISTRICT SUPERINTENDENT OF WICHITA DISTRICT, 2002–2005; DISTRICT SUPERINTENDENT OF WICHITA EAST DISTRICT, 2005–2009

Being a district superintendent has been one of the most rewarding and challenging ministries I have experienced. I served three different districts and hundreds of churches and pastors. Overall, I enjoyed my ministry as a DS. I was the first African American woman to serve as a DS in the Kansas West Conference.

However, there were such difficult times that I wondered if I would or could continue being in ministry!

I served one year in the Salina District, north of Wichita. I loved that time in my first district with amazing churches and pastors. The drawback is that my family—my husband and our four children—remained in Wichita while I lived in Salina. I made the commitment to itinerate, and I was totally open to moving—even if it meant leaving my family. I felt like my children were in good hands with their father, and they were. However, it was difficult being separated from my family.

I did learn from my experience in Salina that all churches have their own personalities, and it reinforced the importance of the role of laity in the local church!

The bishop offered me the Wichita District when my predecessor retired. I immediately said yes to the opportunity of being able to move back with my family! They were in the process of building a new district parsonage, and my family and I were the first occupants. It was during this time that life exploded!

The first years were riddled with clergy misconduct and church conflict cases. I had one season when I had a clergy bring his credentials to my home on a Tuesday and then another pastor on the following Tuesday. I decided not to be home on the next Tuesday, in fear of who might come to my door!

During this season, a colleague suggested that I ask three former district superintendents to meet with me, to consult and provide support, especially during this difficult time. I thank God for that suggestion. That group of three former DSs, all White males, were amazing and supportive and caring, and I'm grateful for their counsel and how they literally saved my life in my time of need. The stress of dealing with church conflict and clergy misconduct can kill a person.

I was involved during a major time of change for our conference. We welcomed a new bishop, voted to downsize districts, and eventually were chosen to be part of going from three annual conferences to one (Kansas West, Kansas East, and Nebraska). So many changes!

I led our delegation in 2004 when we were to receive a new bishop.

In 2006, I turned fifty and got a divorce! It was a very difficult time in my life. Going through divorce as a clergyperson is not easy, and as a DS, it was very difficult. However, I'm grateful for all of the support I received from the bishop and cabinet and colleagues. My ex and I are friends, and our divorce was friendly, but it was still hard!

I ran for bishop twice. These experiences in 2008 and 2012 gave me some insight and revelations about how good some folks can be and how bad, mean, and evil other folks can be. Someone said, after the South Central Jurisdictional meeting in 2008, that the only difference between our election process and that of our nation is that we pray before we stab you in the back. All I could say was "Amen!"

I made it to a runoff with the other candidate for the third bishop to be elected, but I lost. To this day, we have yet to elect a Black female as bishop in the SCJ! One day, Lord!

SEVENTH APPOINTMENT:
2009–2012, SENIOR PASTOR OF TRINITY
HEIGHTS UMC, NEWTON, KANSAS

I was appointed to Trinity Heights UMC, a great church and appointment! It was a good-sized church, financially healthy, and a leader in the community. It was the type of appointment one would expect someone coming off the cabinet to receive. I was excited. I was their first African American and woman to serve as pastor. I had good ministry there. We added a second service, rebuilt a playground for all abled children, and stayed healthy financially.

However, things did not turn out as I had hoped they would. Even though I had a lot of experience, my administrative gifts weren't enough to sustain me. I also was in denial about my diagnosis of ADHD, which I didn't come to terms with until my next appointment. Because of the complication of that reality and other things I didn't realize, plans were in place to have me move in 2012.

I discerned to make another run for the episcopacy, but it was an unsuccessful run. However, I felt good about being able to come back to my appointment, having answered a call from God to give it another try. When I returned from the 2012 SCJ conference, I didn't know that by the time August 2012 ended, I would be out of my appointment and provided a paid vacation until the cabinet could find me another appointment!

That was the hardest experience in my ministry career. I seriously contemplated taking on a third career. I was an electrical engineer before going into ministry full-time. I was being accused of being "an angry Black woman" for sharing from the pulpit how disappointed I was that folks would ask visitors to move from "their seats." I said, "I never thought I'd pastor a church where members would say that to visitors!" Needless to say, I went into depression. I participated in vacation Bible school, knowing that I would be leaving, but the church did not know it yet. I served Communion, remembering scriptures about how we are to come to the Lord's table. I had to move, not knowing where I was going to go. It was a very dark time!

I thank God that He looked out for me! I'm grateful for a colleague who lived in the same town. She provided me with a listening ear and care and support through it all! It took some time, but I am mostly over my anger and hurt!

EIGHTH APPOINTMENT:
2012–2016, ASSOCIATE PASTOR OF CONGREGATIONAL CARE, UNITED METHODIST CHURCH OF THE RESURRECTION, LEAWOOD, KANSAS

I thank God for the opportunity to come on staff at the Church of the Resurrection. This was a place where I have been able to be healed, reclaim my identity, and start on the road to discerning where God is leading me!

The DS called and said there was an appointment on staff at Resurrection in congregational care. I was asked if I would be open to it! When I heard the words, my Spirit leaped within me, reminding me of Elizabeth's encounter with Mary, the mother of Jesus. My spirit was very, very low. This appointment has given me life. Again, I thank God for this opportunity that was made available to me.

Resurrection is a different level of ministry—with the large amount of people that we provide care for—and it is dynamic and vital. We aren't perfect, but it is a great place to be.

There is an obvious question that I'm sure others may have, and I have asked myself, "How do I really feel about being on staff as an associate pastor (with about seventeen others) when I have served as a DS and a senior pastor?" I believe I am in the place that I need to be at this time in my life and career. I do miss the preaching, although I have opportunities to preach and teach. I do miss being in the role of senior pastor, but I do have responsibility for my portion of the congregation, and that has been sufficient for such a time as now.

I was appointed to a church that allowed me to continue providing ministry and living out my calling—while healing from a situation that could have taken my life. I love serving here.

The opportunities for ministry are unlimited. My colleagues are amazing. The senior pastor is the real deal, and I'm enjoying all that is happening here.

Something else amazing happened in my time here at Resurrection. I ran for the 2016 delegation for our newly formed Great Plains Conference, and I was elected! This was amazing, especially in light of the fact that our senior pastor was elected first. It is unusual for more than one person to be elected from one church as delegates. However, I thank God that the connections, relationships, and my reputation helped me get elected—against other odds! I don't take that for granted. It is a testimony that justice can prevail—even in the face of injustice!

I don't know what the immediate future holds for me, but I do know that God will be with me every step of the way!

3. Do you see any of your life stories depicted in the lives of the saints in the Bible? Was it helpful to see yourself in scripture as you journeyed in your appointments?

Elizabeth and Mary's encounter came to mind immediately when the DS asked about my next appointment. I felt a quickening in my spirit.

I also relate to Joseph, speaking to his brothers in Genesis 50, when he told them that what they meant for evil, God turned it for the good! Thanks be to God!

It is always helpful to see my story in scripture because God always shows up! I need that reassurance in my life!

4. If you were the first Black woman, or among the firsts, in any of your appointments, state those firsts, and tell the stories. What words of wisdom would you pass on to others who may become pioneers during their ministry?

In every appointment I have had, except here at the Church of the Resurrection, I have been the first Black woman to serve.

What words of wisdom would you pass on to others who may become pioneers during their ministry?

- Love God's people anyway!
- Be yourself. There is always room to make changes and adjustments, but don't compromise who you are! God created you to be you!
- Be careful. There are wolves in sheep's clothing!

5. In hindsight, how could the annual conference and/or other UM personnel be more helpful when assigning Black clergywomen as firsts in a given area of ministry?

- I think we need to be open about the reality of adjustments that will be made when a Black clergywoman is being appointed for the first time. The reality is that there are always adjustments that are made when there is a change of a pastor, regardless of who the outgoing and/or incoming pastor is. However, because of the reality of being Black in America, and being a Black female, putting everything on the table is important. It will hopefully give the pastor and the church a chance to be successful.
- Black clergywomen are gifts to the church! When we are all able to fully utilize the gifts and graces God has blessed us with, all can be well!

6. What personal gifts and graces have been assets to you during your years of ministry? Be specific and relate how they have been helpful.

- Singing has been a great asset. Music can soothe in many situations. I sing at visits that I make. I participate in choirs as I am able. I sometimes incorporate singing when I speak. Singing has been a bridge for me to connect with my churches and people.
- Growing up in Detroit and living in predominantly White neighborhoods and schools has given me the ability to

interact with White people. I have been able to lean upon my upbringing to take the mystery away from working in cross-racial appointments.

- I truly love people where they are and for who they are. I know that I have worth and believe that about others—that comes through in my relationships and interactions.
- I'm a good listener and observer. This has helped me in all situations in my ministry.

7. List any particular accomplishments or honors conferred during your years of ministry.

- 2019, 2016, 2012, 2008, 2004: Elected as general delegate.
- 2004: Led the general delegation.
- 2016, 2012, 2008, 2004, 2000: Jurisdictional Delegate.
- 2004–2012: General Board of Higher Education and Ministry (GBHEM) Board Member.
- 2008, 2012: South Central Episcopal candidate.
- Served on the Transition Committee to Become One Conference (Kansas West, Kansas East, and Nebraska.)
- District superintendent, Salina District.
- District superintendent, Wichita District.
- District superintendent, Wichita East District.

CHAPTER SIX

Bishop Sharma Denise Lewis

Resident Bishop of Virginia Annual Conference

Conference: Virginia Annual Conference

City: Glen Allen, Virginia

Age: 53

Year accepted the call to
ordained ministry: 1994

Year Ordained: 2002

PHASE 1

1. *Recall significant events in your life and society, by decades, beginning
with year 1-10, 10-20, etc., until the year you accepted the call to
ordained ministry, even if your earlier years were not in a Christian
setting. List any songs that were formative in the life events you include
in your stories.*

YEARS 1–10

I was born in 1963, and I remember my parents sharing with me when
I was five, that right after I was born, President John F. Kennedy was

killed. Actually, the day President Kennedy got shot, my mother was in the doctor's office with me. I was a sickly baby, and while we were in the doctor's office, the news broke on the television that President Kennedy had been assassinated. I remember my mother saying that there was an eeriness and sadness that came over the office when that was happening. People were crying and in disbelief. I don't remember any of that—I just remember mother rehearsing the story.

In 1968, Martin Luther King Jr. was assassinated. I remember my parents rehearsing the story and saying that Black people and White people were affected when that happened. My mother said, "People were numb, people were mad or angry, and people were sad." My mother was the president of the local chapter of the NAACP, and I remember her saying that the NAACP members got together. People were crying and trying to figure out how they would properly mourn the death of a great leader. I remember her saying that people were meeting and trying to figure out how they were going to go to Atlanta to be a part of the homegoing service.

My parents were business owners in Statesboro, Georgia. My father was a bartender in the Statesboro Country Club, but he always said that his desire was to own his own business or businesses and send all his five children to college.

My parents were also very active in the whole area of social justice. I was raised in the early years, from 1963 to 1973, in the real forefront of social justice. After my dad had worked at the Statesboro Country Club for about ten years, he opened his first business, which was a convenience store. Our convenience store was strategically set in what would be considered the middle of Statesboro. You would have to pass my parent's store on Blitch Street to connect to the White area and the Black area.

I remember being raised working at the store, and many, many people—Black people and White people—came to my parents' store. My parents were always very conversational and very relational. Since my mother was the local president of the NAACP, and because my dad was a businessman, local folks would come when there were any issues of injustice. People would come and sit at my parents' door and talk to my mom and/or my dad to figure out what they needed to do. I remember my mother and father, in many, many instances, helping the least of these from a social justice perspective.

In my first ten formative years, my parents' business was a hub, and it seemed like everybody who had a problem would come to my parents.

My parents were also very active in our church, Brannen Chapel United Methodist Church, in Statesboro, Georgia. I was born into a Christian family and reared in the church, and I was baptized at six months old. Consequently, the family business and my family were rocks in the community. My dad had broken some barriers as the town bartender who had made it. He was one of the first Black men to own his own business in Statesboro on Blitch Street.

YEARS 10–20

The 1970s and 1980s included my elementary and high school years. I went to Marvin Pittman Laboratory School, which was an interesting name for an elementary school. Marvin Pittman Laboratory School was connected to Georgia Southern College (now Georgia Southern University.) Georgia Southern was known for educating teachers, and Georgia Southern students who were majoring in education would do their student teaching at Marvin Pittman.

I attended there from first grade through ninth grade. It was a predominantly White school with a few Blacks. A few other ethnic cultures were in attendance, but it was mainly a Black and White school.

One of the things that was very crucial in my life, and when people ask me about my social justice stance, relates back to my elementary and high school days. My sisters who were fourteen, twelve, ten, and eight years older than my brother and I integrated the school system so that my brother and I (who were four years apart) would reap the benefits. Of course, there was a lot of argument as to whether or not integration was good. I did excel. I was not just an average student, but I was an A/B student and received a lot of honors.

After Marvin Pittman Laboratory School, I went to Statesboro High for tenth, eleventh, and twelfth. Statesboro High was an integrated school by that time, and I was very active in the school. During that time, the schools had what was called "grade-level," "college-bound," or vocational-bound" classes. I was in all the college-bound classes. We had three levels, and I was level 3, which was the college-bound level.

My mother would always say, "Is level 3 good?"

I responded, "Yeah, Mama. I'm college bound."

"Why not level 1?" My mother could not understand the different levels of the school.

YEARS 20–30

In 1981, I graduated from Statesboro High and entered Mercer University in Macon, Georgia. I earned a Bachelor of Science degree in biology and a minor in chemistry. I desired to go to medical school, but I was not successful in getting in the first two times. Both times, I was put on the waiting list.

After college, I moved to Washington, DC and tried to get a job. With a degree in biology, I tried to get a job at the National Institutes of Health, but I ended up working for an education firm. I still had a strong desire to go into medicine.

To continue to strengthen my portfolio, I decided to go to graduate school. My desire was to do research and be an MD/PhD. I ended up going to the University of West Georgia, and I received a MS in molecular biology, while I was strengthening my MCAT scores, the national test to get into medical school, and reapplied to medical school.

I applied to medical school for the second time and was wait-listed. I then moved to Atlanta and worked at Emory University, Morehouse School of Medicine, and Morehouse College, doing research. When it was time to apply to medical school for a third time, I had a "crucial conversation" with my aunt. A United Methodist minister, she shared with me that she had watched my life and my progression and felt that I had a call to ministry. At dinner one night, she said, "I know that you have applied to medical school two times, and you are in the process of applying again."

I said, "Yes, it will be the third time."

Every time that I applied, I got on the waiting list, and if you know anything about the medical school process, you either get in, or they put your name on a waiting list, or you are denied admittance. As people decide not to enter that medical school, if you are on the waiting list, your name is bumped up until you get in or are denied admittance. I was wait-listed twice for medical school, but I never got in.

When I applied to medical school that third time, I had the conversation with my aunt. She was really encouraging me to seek God about my purpose, and she kept saying, "I know that you feel that you are supposed to be a doctor, and I would love for you to be a doctor, but I really do believe that there is something else God has for you."

My aunt and many other people told me they had seen the call on my life. I would say, "Well, when I see it or feel it, I will let you all know!"

I am actually the fourteenth pastor in my family, and people are always wondering why I didn't think I was called. I say, "Because I didn't want to accept the call on the legacy of family members. I wanted God to speak to me."

After I had that crucial conversation with my aunt, I went through a process for about a year. During that time, I really truly sought the Lord. I talked to various people I trusted, sought wise counsel, and none of them tried to convince me. They all kept saying, "Keep praying, keep seeking, and keep your heart open to what God is saying."

The pastor at Ben Hill encouraged me to go to Gammon Theological Seminary for a course called "Call to Ministry." During the weekend course, professors and students would expose you to the seminary life. As I was sitting in that class, I literally heard the voice of God saying, "You will be here one day!"

I said, "OK, that must be God. I know that I'm not hearing things."
"You will be here one day."

I sat on it, and I began to talk to the people I trusted at Ben Hill.

Again and again, people would say, "I really think you have a call on your life."

I responded to the questionable call by becoming more active in church. I chaired different ministries, I was in young adult ministry, I participated in vision ministry (a ministry of social service/social justice,) and I did everything but pulpit ministry. It wasn't that I didn't feel that I could be a preacher, but I just didn't see it for me. Also, I had a strong passion about going to medical school.

Another pastor was appointed to the church, and I asked him to pray with me.

He encouraged me by saying, "God will tell you—be open."

After a year of honestly seeking the Lord, praying, fasting, and seeking wise counsel, I got my answer. On February 13, 1994, the sermon at Ben Hill United Methodist Church was "Are You Called?" The text was from Ephesians 4:11: "Some are called to be pastors, apostles..." Following the sermon, he extended an altar call for prayer and an invitation for Christian discipleship. I went to the altar and knelt because I had been seeking God for a year.

The voice of God clearly said, "Go! Preach My Word!"

I knew then, beyond a shadow of a doubt, and I started crying uncontrollably.

As I was kneeling at the altar, the preacher handed me the microphone and whispered, "Is there something you would like to say?"

I stood up and turned around, and to this day, I do not remember how the people moved from their pews to stand behind me. Three-quarters of the congregation was standing behind me with smiles and tears. I stood before my Ben Hill family and said, "I heard the voice of God today, right here, and the voice of God said, 'Go. Preach My Word!' I want you all to know that I will be going to seminary and accepting my call to ministry today."

By September 1994, I started seminary—and the rest is history!

Songs that were formative in the life events you include in your stories.

There is one hymn that I love, and it reminds me of the power of Christ. I always talk about "Blessed Assurance" in my sermons or as I am witnessing. The refrain says, "This is my story, this is my song, praising my Savior all the day long." I truly believe that everyone has a unique story and a unique path with the Lord. Nobody can take that from you, and that's why I think that hymn is so powerful: "This is my (personal) story, this is my (personal) song, praising my Savior all the day long."

That relationship with God has always been a major, formidable part of my life. I have been United Methodist all my life. When I was twelve years old, I accepted Christ in Brannen Chapel, a small-town church. After the pastor preached his sermon, he would do a natural "opening of the doors of the church." I walked down the aisle, and when I got in front of the pastor, instead of him taking me into the church—as I had seen him do with many, many adults—he leaned over and whispered, "Do you know what you are doing?"

I whispered, "Yes, I do! I want to join this church, and I want to accept Jesus Christ as my personal Lord and Savior." I told him that I had already had a conversation with my parents about what I was doing. At twelve years old, I felt the presence of God saying, "Go," and then I went down the aisle.

At twelve years old, I began to deepen my relationship with the Lord. I went through confirmation, and I was very active in my church. Every Saturday, I would go over to a Sunday school teacher's house to help her with the lessons. When I was fourteen, she asked the pastor if I could teach my own vacation Bible class. I was thrilled! My entire upbringing had always been in the church, but being a pastor or a bishop was the farthest thing from my mind. I was just a layperson who loved the Lord, who loved to serve the Lord, who loved to teach, and eventually loved to preach because God called me.

"Blessed Assurance" is one of my favorite hymns. It helped shape my life and my ministry. I draw on it even now: "This is my story, this is my song, praising my Savior, all the day long!" The praise part is also very powerful because I think music is a universal language, and I love to praise God. I love to experience different worship services. I say, "I can praise God by myself. I can praise God in the car. I can praise God in church. I don't need a choir. I don't need a praise team. I don't need anybody but me and the Lord." Even when I get into my own prayer closet, I'll bring in my iPhone and sit and praise God, literally by myself, because I know the goodness of God in my life, in my family's lives, and other folks' lives.

2. *Recall the people who significantly contributed to your Christian formation up to the acceptance of the call. Tell the stories of how they influenced your life.*

Let me first start with my parents. My parents were very formidable in my spiritual formation, and I covered their influence in a previous question.

Secondly, my aunt—who accepted her call very late—was a pastor in the United Methodist Church of the South Georgia Conference. She influenced me a lot, along with my parents. My aunt lived next door to us and took care of my grandmother on my maternal side. I saw her as a visionary. I would also say that I gleaned a pastor's heart from my aunt. I would, as a child, travel with her as she served communion and made hospital and nursing home visits. I would even go to class with her to the "Course of Study" classes at Emory-Candler School of Theology. Interestingly, more than twenty years later, I studied with my aunt's professor.

I was influenced by the Sunday school teacher I helped on Saturdays with the lessons on Sundays and later recommended that I teach my own VBS class. The pastor who was not sure that I knew what I was doing when I joined the church and gave my life to Christ consented for me to teach my own VBS class. That acceptance of my teaching gift at age fourteen had a profound effect on my life.

When I was a member of Ben Hill, the same preacher who was preaching when I accepted my call was also very formidable in my upbringing in the young adult phase. While I was at Ben

Hill, as a young adult (somewhat running from my call), he was the clergyperson assigned to singles and young adult ministries.

Recently, we were laughing because I said, "You know, it's amazing how long I've known you and your wife, and the reason why I don't have a husband even to this day, even though I desire one, is that on Friday nights, instead of me being a young adult and partying, I was over at your house for thirteen weeks studying how to pray." All seven of us who studied with them on Friday nights are in ministry! That prayer class was very instrumental in developing my strong spiritual discipline of prayer that I have carried in my ministry.

Another person who greatly influenced me was one of the pastors of Ben Hill UMC in Atlanta, who was later elected bishop. He influenced me and encouraged me to go to Gammon Seminary for the weekend class on "The Call to Ministry."

A lot of men influenced my life in ministry, but I was blessed to see women—my aunt, my mother, the Sunday school teacher, and other women—who equally influenced my call to ministry. Some people grow up without ever seeing women in ministry. I am blessed to be the fourteenth pastor in my family. I have aunts who are Apostolic pastors and Pentecostal pastors, and one aunt was a United Methodist pastor.

3. Recall the people/events that significantly served to deter your affirming the call to ordained ministry.

When I was twelve years old, I walked forward to join and make the public profession of Jesus Christ, but the pastor said, "Do you know what you are doing?" If there was ever a time that I would have gotten a bad taste in my mouth for church or clergy, it would have been then. I believe it did not scar my journey because the same pastor, two years later, agreed to let me teach my own VBS class at age fourteen.

Another opportunity that could have deterred my affirming the call—with no offense to the Baptist Church—was when I was in graduate school at the University of West Georgia. From 1986 until

1988, there really was no United Methodist Church that was close to campus. There was one UMC, but since I didn't have a car, I couldn't really go there. I was working on my master's degree, and I would go into the lab early on Sunday mornings or during the day. I never could get a ride to the Methodist church, but a Baptist church was close enough that I could walk.

In that Baptist church, I noticed that there were no females in the pulpit. When women would speak, they would have to speak from the floor, but men would speak from the pulpit. The women were only allowed to teach Sunday school, usher, and speak from the floor. I was a Baptist for a year, but after seeing the inequality of women, I ran back to the Methodist church—and I have never left.

4. When you received the call to ordained ministry, did you respond yes immediately and take appropriate action? Why or why not?

Well, the answer to that is yes. I wrestled, talked, prayed, fasted, and sought wise counsel for a year. When God spoke on February 13, 1994, at Ben Hill, I said yes to God and yes to the church. I went to seminary in September 1994, and it took me five years to finish. I paid for the first three years because I didn't want much debt. I went part-time and still worked full-time. The last two years, I quit all of my jobs and went full-time to seminary. In my fifth year of seminary, I was offered a position at Ben Hill as a student minister of children's ministry.

5. What was your occupation when you received the call, and what effect did it have on your response?

I worked as a research scientist in endocrinology. Secondly, I worked at Scientific Games in Alpharetta, Georgia, as an ink chemist. I worked in the Department of Research and Development, which prevents tampering with lottery tickets. I didn't play the lottery, but I worked for the lottery—yes so, that was kind of bizarre. Neither the job nor occupation had any influence in my accepting the call.

6. If you did not take immediate action to the call, recall the thinking/ rationale that caused resistance to your immediate response.

I did respond after I clearly heard and understood God saying He wanted me to preach, and I have no regrets!

7. What occurred that enabled you to overcome the resistance to answering the call?

I did not resist the call once I heard the voice of God. I would not respond to the call until I was sure God was calling me.

8. What was the time frame between receiving the call and saying yes with appropriate action?

Receiving the call and taking the appropriate action, I wrestled for a year, and then I answered the call in February 1994, and I began the process to enter seminary in September 1994.

9. What role did the church play in your answering or not answering the call immediately?

When I was trying to discern if I had been called, I was blessed to have clergy and laity at Ben Hill who listened and prayed with me. When I did accept the call, I had people who affirmed the call because on that day when I turned around and saw all those people standing behind me, at the altar, it was quite an affirmation. The church played a powerful role in affirming my call.

10. Were there any spiritual disciplines that played a role in your resistance or acceptance of the call? Tell the stories.

As I was seeking God and trying to discern my call, I read scripture, prayed, and fasted. I studied about fasting, and I took a thirteen-week class on prayer.

11. *In retrospect, how do you see God's hand at work in your life that prepared you for ordained ministry?*

In retrospect, what prepared me was my opportunity to be a student minister of children's ministry at Ben Hill. I had more than one hundred kids in junior church. I had more kids in the junior church than many churches had in their main church service. I had to learn how to worship with little people and keep their attention. I had to break down the Word so that little people would understand it. Also, I had to learn to work with a children's ministry team, parents, and volunteers.

12. *When you accepted the call to ministry, what was the response from persons in your life?*

Ben Hill people were elated. My parents, initially, were shocked because they wanted me to go to medical school. However, my family affirmed it. They knew that once God spoke, I was going to pursue my call. My aunt, a United Methodist pastor, was elated.

PHASE 2

1. *Tell the story of your first three years while meeting the requirements necessary for elder's or deacon's ordination or for local pastor's requirements. What were some of your struggles and victories as you pursued answering the call?*

- *Share your stories with the Board(s) of Ordained Ministry. In what ways were they helpful? Did you have any identifiable issues that you were told to improve upon?*
- *If you were assigned to a church(s) during those first three years, what relationships did you have with the parishioners and the community?*
- *When you attended seminary or licensing school, what were your experiences with faculty, staff, and peers? Include the specific years?*

I was ordained as provisional deacon in 1999 under the Board of Ordained Ministry in the North Georgia Annual Conference. It was a wonderful blessing. I took the written test and passed it the first time. During the process, many people had struggles, including African Americans, but I was fortunate to have a mentor who quizzed me and guided me through the process. It helped tremendously, and I had no issues when I went before the board. The content and grammar were on point for the paperwork.

My seminary training started in 1994 at Gammon Seminary of ITC in Atlanta. I attended three years part-time and two years full-time. I had great relationships with the professors. I was especially close to three professors who were United Methodists. ITC housed six denominational schools, which was helpful. We were exposed to other denominations with various worship, preaching, and organizational styles.

My peers and I had very good relationships. In fact, I recently preached for one of my Baptist peers. Some of the seminary students went to the Holy Land, underwritten by a grant, in 2000. Nearly twenty years later, some of us are still connected through social media, traveling together to various venues, and shared preaching. Somehow, we managed to stick together. Two of us are now bishops, and seven are district superintendents.

2. *Share your stories of each individual appointment since beginning the process for ordination until 2016. Include the following:*

- *What lessons did you learn from each appointment?*
- *What meaningful relationships were established? Include personal, professional, and church member relationships.*
- *What was your personal and church financial state? Relate any successes or challenges you faced in each appointment.*
- *Were there any personal events that affected your ministry (weddings, deaths, or illnesses?)*

FIRST APPOINTMENT:
PASTOR OF CHILDREN'S MINISTRY, BEN
HILL UMC, ATLANTA, GEORGIA

I was children's pastor for four and a half years at Ben Hill. Ben Hill was a large congregation, so children's ministry was large with almost one hundred children. Through junior church, I worked with parents and children. I laid a foundation for children that was relevant and fostered age-appropriate Christian development. I also designed a curriculum that enhanced relationships with the parents. Relationships with the children and parents grew very deep and meaningful. The children's ministry grew under my leadership.

I developed professional relationships with other staff associates, including ten clergy.

Ben Hill was a large African American Church with no financial problems.

My personal financial status was maintained by a stipend from Ben Hill and working part-time as a chemist.

No events affected my appointment. However, while being active in the Black Methodist for Church Renewal (BMCR), I experienced other Black clergy as advocates.

At Ben Hill, I learned people are valuable, and I developed long-term relationships. Some of them even came to hear me preach twenty years later.

SECOND APPOINTMENT:
ASSOCIATE PASTOR OF EVANGELISM AT BEN
HILL UM CHURCH, ATLANTA, GEORGIA

As associate pastor, I was actively involved in developing ministries that were specifically designed to take the Gospel outside the walls of the church. We developed good relationships within the community as we took "Jesus to the streets" with Bible study and door-to-door evangelism.

Since many people in the community didn't know Jesus Christ, we had to break down the meaning of Christian terms. As the church continued to grow, the team had to be intentional in evangelizing the community.

The professors in seminary became my mentors and taught me self-care and a balanced life must be maintained. They also shared that the "ministry of presence" was critical in some situations where one would sit by the bed of a person, hold their hand, and even cry with them.

During those years, Ben Hill was strong in BMCR, and the General Church started the "Strengthening the Black Church" emphasis. Ben Hill became a Congregational Resource Center (CRC) that served to train other Black churches in effectiveness.

THIRD APPOINTMENT:
1994–2004, SENIOR ASSOCIATE PASTOR, BEN HILL UM CHURCH, ATLANTA, GEORGIA

I utilized many administrative skills and was responsible for leadership training. I was responsible for the multi-clergy staff and was moving up the ranks as a clergywoman. Ben Hill saw leadership skills in me and placed me in positions of authority. I was being prepared to pastor my own church. Meaningful relationships of trust were built with children and adults.

FOURTH APPOINTMENT:
2004–2007, SENIOR PASTOR, POWERS FERRY, UMC, MARIETTA, GEORGIA

I was the first woman and first Black pastor at Powers Ferry in fifty years. The ministry took a good turn, and spiritual disciplines came alive.

In the Anglo environment, there were issues of sexism and racism. Some people left, and some would not shake hands. Ethnic diversity began to occur as Asian, Black, and biracial couples began to join. However, this was problematic for some members at Powers Ferry.

I had to depend on God as never before. I had to seriously deal with rejection. Thankfully, the district superintendent was supportive. In reflection, those times helped strengthen my character and made me strong as a Black person. I had to understand their culture, learn their system, and learn how to preach to their hearts. I was led by the Holy Spirit not to make the ministry about race. These were God's people, and I was called to preach the Word of God. During this time, my spiritual discipline of prayer was deepened. I learned to pray more (cry to God) while God was building my character. Now that I am bishop of the Virginia Conference, which is primarily Caucasian, I see my growth at Powers Ferry as part of my preparation for bishop.

At Powers Ferry, I started a prayer ministry, confirmation classes, and women's ministries.

The DS wisely said, "Don't go after masses but after the remnant." There were twenty people in Bible study, and this changed my perspective about ministry. I saw the people change when I surrendered to God. The ministry was not about race or sex; it was about God and God's people.

There were very few personal relationships established, but two strong relationships were formed with the youth pastor and the leader of the children's ministry.

The financial status of the church included an endowment. The church had 175 worship attendees. The church was an older congregation, and thirty-seven people died during my tenure. This greatly affected the financial status of the church.

My personal finances were affected when I was given a cut in pay. With all the deaths and personal rejection, I sought counsel from a Christian therapist.

FIFTH APPOINTMENT:
2007–2010, PASTOR OF WESLEY CHAPEL, McDONOUGH, GEORGIA

Wesley Chapel was a phenomenal ministry. I was the first Black woman in a Black church that was 140 years old. The church began to grow in diversity. The ministry was not about race or culture. More than 650 people joined the church, including more than seventy professions of faith. The church became more financially sound and moved from one to three services.

The church honored my leadership with an increase in salary. Many lasting relationships were formed, and several people entered professional ministry under my leadership. The church was everything I wanted. They didn't care that I was a woman or Black. They wanted a pastor to lead from the front and be present in the community.

I received the Conference Denman Award and the C. Ross Freeman Award. Our church started many new ministries. God showed me the fruit of my labor.

Challenges occurred in developing ministries for women, young people in the community, and singles ministry. The church doubled in worship attendance, which increased my need to provide self-care and develop more staff. With the influx of new people, we were challenged to successfully merge old traditions with new ideas—so all would feel included and cared for.

SIXTH APPOINTMENT:
2010–2016, DISTRICT SUPERINTENDENT OF
ATLANTA/DECATUR/OXFORD DISTRICTS

As a DS, I had oversight over twenty-five thousand laity, sixty-three churches, and 123 pastors, which consisted of 65 percent Anglo, 35 percent Black, and 1 percent Hispanic constituents.

I was the first woman and the first Black clergywoman to serve in the position. Under my leadership, the district apportionments increased from 85 percent to 92 percent. Our focus was to collaborate, equip, empower, and provide conflict-management training. I was able to develop relationships with the bishop, district superintendents, clergy colleagues, and laity of the district.

District financials were great, which stemmed from sale of

properties. Grants were awarded to churches to help them build their facilities.

Personally, my financial status was a raise in salary to the DS level.

I ran for bishop while a delegate to the General Conference in 2012, but I was not elected. I was active in BMCR and National Black Clergy Women (BCW), and I worked extensively with the General Church and the Southeastern Jurisdiction (SEJ).

SEVENTH ASSIGNMENT:
IN 2016, I WAS ELECTED BISHOP ON THE FIRST BALLOT.

My consecration was special as my mother, two sisters, brothers, and friends watched this historic event. Unfortunately, my dad, a sister, and an aunt passed before my election.

I was well received by the Virginia delegation. When I was installed at a service in Virginia, there were many family and friends as well as members of the Virginia Conference. More than a thousand people were in attendance. It was an awesome service.

3. *Do you see any of your life stories depicted in the lives of the saints in the Bible? Was it helpful to see yourself in scripture as you journeyed in your appointment?*

I had to research the scriptures for discerning my call. I could relate to Jeremiah and Isaiah.

4. *If you were the first Black woman, or among the firsts, in any of your appointments, state those firsts, and tell the stories. What words of wisdom would you pass on to others who may become pioneers during their ministry?*

- First Black woman to serve as senior associate pastor at Ben Hill UMC.
- First Black and first clergywoman at Powers Ferry UMC.

- First Black clergywoman at Wesley Chapel UMC.
- First Black clergywoman DS in Atlanta/Decatur/Oxford District.
- First African American clergywoman elected as Bishop in the Southeastern Jurisdiction.
- First Black female bishop of the Virginia Annual Conference.

What words of wisdom would you pass on to others who may become pioneers during their ministry?

- For most of my career, I have been first in my appointments. God can trust me with power and trailblazing. I have a strong work ethic, and I carry myself in ways that help others. I know that doors have not opened by accident. I try to live in a fashion that I will be remembered positively.
- Be sure to remember you are called by God. Elections and appointments are how we live the call to ministry.
- Revisit your call when the way gets difficult.
- Make sure to practice spiritual disciplines.
- Live a balanced life by attending to soul, body, and spirit.
- Love God's people genuinely—and they will love you back.
- Get to know your people and cast a vision. Ministry is good common sense plus the anointing of the Holy Spirit.

5. In hindsight, how could the annual conference and/or other UM personnel be more helpful when signing Black clergywomen as firsts in a given area of ministry?

- Know the personal and professional gifts of the Black clergywoman and match them with the needs and strengths of the church.
- Give support before and during the appointment.
- Give training to SPRC before the appointment.
- Lay the groundwork with the annual conference and the congregation.

- Create a cross-racial network.
- District and conference personnel should show up for worship sometimes.
- Address complaints head-on.

6. What personal gifts and graces have been assets to you during your years of ministry? Be specific and relate how they have been helpful.

- Administration is one of my assets. I excel in identifying problems and working through them. I look for ways to organize things to address the needs of the ministry more effectively. I seek to work with what I have while searching for additional resources and strategies.
- I look for ways to utilize my faith, which gets tested and tried over and over again. I try to see how God is working in the situation, and sometimes I have to step out in blind faith.
- I pastor by building relationships and leading from a shepherd's heart.

7. List any particular accomplishments or honors conferred during your years of ministry.

- Denman Award.
- C. Ross Freeman Award.
- Gammon Alumni Trailblazer Award.
- Delta Sigma Theta Torch Award.
- Powers Ferry Church grew numerically.
- Wesley Chapel doubled in worship and paid 100 percent of its apportionment.
- While DS of Atlanta/Decatur/Oxford districts, the apportionments increased from 85–92 percent in six years.
- Elected bishop 2016: The first Black woman in the Southeastern Jurisdiction Conference.
- First Black women to lead the North Georgia delegation in 2012 and 2016 for the General and Jurisdictional Conferences.

CHAPTER SEVEN

Rev. Edna Mae Morgan

Church: Hawley Memorial United
Methodist and Wesley United Methodist
City: Pine Bluff, Arkansas
Conference: Arkansas
Age: 65 years old
Accepted the call to ordained ministry:
1990 (in the UM Church)
Year Ordained: 2007

PHASE 1

1. *Recall significant events in your life and society, by decades, beginning with year 1-10, 10-20, etc., until the year you accepted the call to ordained ministry, even if your earlier years were not in a Christian setting. List any songs that were formative in the life events you include in your stories.*

YEARS 1-10

When I looked back at these first years, I remember learning to read, and to me, that was one of the most fascinating things. I would also go with my mother to her school. She taught elementary school, so from first grade all the way through to twelfth grade, she would take us, every year, at the beginning of the year, to meet all of her students, and she would take us to each student's home.

That was the beginning of knowing what it means to give back into the community and to care for those you don't know. My mother was very meticulous about that. She really felt that each child was important, each child was significant, and if she took her own children to meet them, then the parents would know that she loved their children as well. She had children of her own, and she understood this interaction was important in establishing good relationships. That was such a wonderful time for my family and the families in her classes.

The community that I lived in was a village. I remember walking home one day, and we passed by a neighbor's house about a block away. That neighbor had beautiful flowers. Well, we picked her flowers, and we weren't supposed to. She had beautiful roses and daffodils, and I don't know what else she had, but by the time we got home, we were in big trouble because she had called our moms. We had to take the flowers back, and when we came back home, we got a spanking. The village I grew up in was so wonderful because everyone looked out for everyone else's children. Yes, we had some seniors in the neighborhood who would tell on us, but that was a good thing because we couldn't get away with anything. We learned at an early age how to make good choices.

YEARS 10–20

That was the time when I really began to learn what it meant to serve God. When I was twelve years old, I accepted Christ as my personal Savior. I had been baptized as a baby. I had also listened to all the different topics that we had for confirmation, and one directive stood out to me the most: "Now, you've got to be used by God."

My Sunday school teacher was also my godmother, and I kept telling her I wanted to do something for Jesus. After several weeks, even after we were confirmed before the congregation, she said to my mother, "I've got to find something for her to do because she keeps asking me."

I became a candy striper at twelve years old, and I've been working in nursing homes ever since. I began using my hands to help braid hair, brush hair, write letters, and read the Bible and other books, or newspapers to them. Since then, I have been serving the church in various capacities.

I also learned how to play piano very well. I started when I was five years old, but I played so well that I played for Sunday school. When our organist was late, I was able to play for church. I really enjoyed my childhood. We had a wonderful minister, and we were surrounded with lots of love and care. Everything centered around the church. It was a fantastic childhood. We had our birthday parties, youth fellowship, and block parties at the church. I was close to God doing so many activities in the church.

We had a wonderful time at church, and I really enjoyed elementary, middle, and high school. I was valedictorian of my high school. I played flute in the band and played piano for the choir. Again, I had a wonderful childhood.

When I was eighteen, I went away to college. I had one of my worst years because my mom died. Nevertheless, it was still good because the community surrounded my family with love, sending us cards and sending me money in college. In Pine Bluff, when we went to the funeral, they surrounded us with so much food and so much love. They even came over to the house for several days.

I lost my mom when I was eighteen and my dad when I was twelve, but things just kept going on because the community and the church were so good to us. They have always been good to us.

YEARS 20–30

I got married at age twenty, dropped out of school, and moved to Millington, Tennessee. I had a scholarship, and I only had one year to finish because I had gone to summer school every year, but I dropped out anyway. My husband was my high school sweetheart and was in the Navy. We started a family. My first daughter was born in 1973, and my husband was assigned to go on the *Kitty Hawk*/West PAC Tour. I stayed with my grandmother in Conway, Arkansas, while he was on the aircraft carrier.

My grandmother came to stay with my sister when my mom died. This time, I went and stayed with her, and I finished at Hendrix College in 1974. I loved that school. It was wonderful, and they were really, really good to me. I had a good time with Granny and all the rest of the family, eating two or three meals and going from house to house. Anyway, it was fun.

When my husband returned, we moved to Silver Springs, Maryland. He attended a Navy school, and I worked at the Farm Cadet Administration in DC. That was fun.

We moved to Okinawa, Japan. That's where my second daughter was born in 1977. We jokingly say, "She was made in Japan!" We always told her that. When she was just a little bitty thing, maybe two or three, my husband said, "Made in Japan is stamped on her butt." She believed it and got really mad one day.

My daughter said, "Mommy, Daddy said it was stamped on my butt, and I don't know what to do about that!" I said, "He was just teasing!" She said, "No, he meant it. He meant it! I know he did!" I had to get him to tell her the truth! It was so funny!

We loved living in Okinawa. It was wonderful learning the Japanese culture. We lived on a base, and on the base, there were people from every nationality you can think of. A good friend of mine was Hispanic and taught me how to cook a lot of Mexican food. On my left was a Filipino family. Down the street, we had Japanese, and then we had Caucasians and African Americans. It was just wonderful living in a multicultural community. Oh, and one of my best friends was from Korea.

We had a marvelous time in that country, which is very much like an African American culture. It is very family-oriented culture, and when they have parties, it is for all of the family. If the party is for a child, everyone goes—moms, dads, aunts, uncles—the same way we do, so it was a lot of fun in Okinawa. In fact, in Okinawa, I played piano for the Catholic and the Protestant services. I had not accepted my call yet.

YEARS 30–40

From Okinawa, we went to California—I believe that it was Los Alamitos—and that was wonderful. I lived four miles from the beach, and I had a wonderful time serving the church. I got very active in church again. I was serving as a Sunday school teacher, and then as the Sunday school superintendent, and I was involved in the choir and praise team. I loved to sing and play, and that was always a wonderful way for me to get involved and learn about the new communities every time we moved. My husband served twenty-two years in the Navy.

I was at a Methodist church when the pastor left the Methodist church. They were going to send him to the desert somewhere, and he would have to leave his other job as a postal officer, so he decided to leave and form the Circle of Joy Bible Church. I left that Methodist church and went with him to the Bible Church and accepted my call to the ministry there. That was in 1988, but we were getting ready to move to Beltsville, Maryland.

I told my husband about my call, and my husband at that time was not going to church. I had a wonderful charismatic friend, an evangelist, and we prayed for him to come back to the Lord. He came back to the Lord, and he accepted his call to ministry. By 1990, both of us had accepted our calls.

List any songs that were formative in your life events you include in your stories.

I learned "Jesus Loves the Little Children" when I was really young, and I loved that song. I just thought it was so beautiful. All the children of the world—Red, Yellow, Black, and White—are precious in His sight. I taught it and sang it to my children. Another formative song was "Jesus Loves Me, This I Know." We sang a lot of hymns since I was head of children's choirs, but those two really stuck in my heart and were very special to me.

One of my favorite verses is from Psalm 91:1 (NIV). "He who dwells in the shelter of the Most High will rest in the shadow of the Almighty." We sang that as a song.

Another favorite verse is from Psalm 27:1 (NIV). "The Lord is my light and my salvation—whom shall I fear?" We also sang this Bible verse as a song.

These are my favorite songs. I could go on forever because I know so many of them, but those are some of my favorites.

2. Recall the people who significantly contributed to your Christian formation up to the acceptance of the call. Tell the stories of how they influenced your life.

My mom taught me how to give back, she taught me the Lord's Prayer and Psalm 23, and she took us to church.

My Sunday school teacher taught me so much about the Bible and so many Bible stories.

The candy striper times were significant. I learned that you should always serve the Lord and that everyone has a gift to serve the Lord.

As I became older, two pastors in California were influential. I received the call in California, but I did not accept that call until we moved to Maryland.

The first pastor said, "We accept women here—whatever God is calling you to do—yes, you can serve!"

The second pastor said, "Well, I'm not surprised. I'm really not! I'm going to make you outreach minister."

This was back in 1988, and it was wonderful. I had pastors who didn't have any problem with my call. They influenced my life by giving me responsibilities and trusting me with those responsibilities. They let me do what God had called me to do. Also, they were not micromanagers. When they saw you were doing a good job, and you were doing what God called you to do, they just left you alone to do it! In fact, I loved working for them a lot more than I liked working for the federal government and all the bureaucracy. The bureaucracy in the federal government is just bureaucracy!

These are the people who significantly contributed to my Christian formation up to the acceptance of the call.

3. Recall the people/events that significantly served to deter your affirming the call to ordained ministry.

I can't think of anyone who deterred it!

I can't think of any events that deterred affirming the call except maybe my daughter's illness because we had to care for her. That was a very emotional time. Our emotions were down as we cared for her. Simultaneously, we tried to keep her positive and motivated. With God's help, we were able to do so! Thank God! He was there for us in those trials—as He always is! We learned to count it all joy, realizing that one day He would make a way of escape for us, which He did. When we came home to Arkansas, she was completely healed! Her healing is a miraculous story! My daughter had a miraculous brain surgery and complete recuperation. Praise God!

We have been able to help so many people as they were going through illnesses because we had a sick daughter. We knew how to be caregivers, and we understood what they were going through. We understood the patients and what they were going through. You can't really walk in anyone's shoes, but we developed a lot more compassion than most because we lived it every day.

4. When you received the call to ordained ministry, did you respond yes immediately and take appropriate action? Why or why not?

I didn't respond by going to seminary right away, and I didn't tell my pastor until the Lord kept disturbing me in the middle of the night and giving me things to write down. Also, when I'd hear a sermon during the day, all the way home, I would be given points to write down. I would write many things in my journal.

I have been writing in journals and diaries since I was five or six years old. I had so many of them, but they got wet. I was going to write a book, but they got soaking wet, and I told my husband to throw them away. He said, "You sure?" I said, "Yes!" I regretted it later on, thinking that I probably could have dried them out. Anyway, I've always journaled.

I didn't pay attention to the call until the Lord just kept bugging me! He kept calling me and putting sermons on my mind. So many thoughts came to my mind. It was absolutely amazing!

I even tried to appease God by saying, "Oh, I'll just start a Bible study at my job." I started a Bible study in California, and it was wonderful. We had a full house.

I was sitting in service, and as the pastor was preaching, all these different ideas came into my mind. I said, "I've got to talk with you, now."

He said, "What's going on?"

I told him, and he laughed. "Yeah, I'm not surprised that you are called into the ministry!" He agreed that God was speaking to me, and He wanted me to preach. The pastor affirmed that God wanted me to be more than a Sunday school superintendent and outreach coordinator. He was tickled and thought it was so funny! I accepted my call after trying to appease God by starting a Bible study at work.

5. *What was your occupation when you received the call, and what effect did it have on your response?*

I was a management analyst, a GS-13, for the federal government. It didn't really have an effect on my response because I had served in lay ministry at all the churches, and I was always a full-time worker. My occupation didn't disturb the call at all.

6. *If you did not take immediate action to the call, recall the thinking/ rationale that caused resistance to your immediate response.*

Well, I did think I couldn't pastor because I was a woman. I thought I wouldn't be accepted. I never had a female pastor growing up in Pine Bluff, Arkansas!

7. What occurred that enabled you to overcome the resistance to answering the call?

I kept getting invited to preach at Women's Day services. Even in Pine Bluff, I was asked to preach. They had a big service like a camp meeting at one of the big churches, and they asked me to preach! I was really shocked, but I preached at that service. I guess I just knew then. I don't think there was a lot of resistance other than not telling the pastor for two years that I was called to the ministry. Isn't that something? I've always felt that I was a minister, but being called to minister as a pastor was a different thing.

8. What was the time frame between receiving the call and saying yes with appropriate action?

I received the call in California in 1988, but I didn't start at Wesley Seminary in Maryland until 1990. I didn't finish seminary because my daughter got sick. I started there, but I finished at the Memphis Theological Seminary in Tennessee.

9. What role did the church play in your answering or not answering the call immediately?

Well, because they kept giving me so many ministerial duties, I felt like I was walking in the call until the Lord kept bugging me with all these different things! God gave me so many things to write about!

The churches in Maryland and California were always receptive of women. As a layperson, I had no problem doing pastoral care, going to hospitals with communion, visiting the sick and shut-ins, going to homes to pray with the sick, and using the anointing oil as I prayed for healing.

The church played a wonderful role with my acceptance of the call. Through the years, the church has extended care, compassion, and love for my family and me. The church was especially loving to our sick daughter. Churches have been so wonderful throughout my journey. One of my previous pastors flew all the way to Dallas to be with us when our daughter was having her brain surgery.

10. *Were there any spiritual disciplines that played a role in your resistance or acceptance of the call? Tell the stories.*

The spiritual discipline of prayer has played a role in my acceptance of the call. I have always been a prayer warrior and have always been very close to God. I learned to pray when I was very young, and I learned to pray for others when I was doing nursing home ministry at twelve years of age! Prayer has been a spiritual discipline that has always played a role in my acceptance of the call.

Another spiritual discipline was journaling. Yes, yes, all my life! All my life, I woke up, did my four-mile walk, came back, did my journaling, read my Bible, read my *Upper Room*, and had my prayer time. It's just a part of my everyday routine. If I miss journaling in the morning, I make sure I do it during my evening prayer time.

The discipline of reading the Bible is the third discipline that has been consistent for many years. Therefore, the disciplines of reading the Bible, praying, and journaling are disciplines that I practice every day.

11. *In retrospect, how do you see God's hand at work in your life that prepared you for ordained ministry?*

I went with my mom when I was really little, met the children in her elementary class, and learned not to meet strangers. God's hand was at work in me. It helped me accept people regardless of their status in life. Some of my mom's students had outdoor toilets. Some had houses that looked like mine, and some did not. We would visit all of them and have a good time with them. When I came to First Methodist Church, and they made me an associate, I was not amazed when they put me in charge of the outreach money that helps pay utilities for people and provide money for them to stay at the Salvation Army. That ministry was given to me because I didn't meet any strangers, and I treated them all with respect because we are all God's children. It didn't matter how they looked, how they smelled, whether they were on alcohol or drugs, or whatever. I was always the one who worked with them and enjoyed it!

I could see God's hand at work at a very young age—when I was in elementary school, when I was a candy striper, and every time I had a part in Christmas or Easter plays. I could see God working as I learned more about God. I could see God working all around me.

My dad was not very active in church, but he would send money. Folks would give him deer, squirrels, and rabbits, and even at home, I was around people from every walk of life. Our neighborhood, an all-Black neighborhood, had some people who were laborers, and others who worked on campuses as teachers or professors. There was a good mix in the neighborhood we lived in, and that was wonderful!

God was preparing me to receive anyone into the body of Christ. God was preparing me to love and extend compassion to anyone. When I was in CPE, some of the people in the hospital had AIDS. I wasn't afraid of them because I wasn't afraid of anybody. I didn't have sense enough to be afraid of anybody because I grew up in a neighborhood where everybody loved everybody. I wasn't even afraid of gang members in Compton, California, where I went to church for four years.

I see God's hand working throughout my life as I was active in the church. I was always a prayer warrior. It was wonderful!

12. *When you accepted the call to ministry, what was the response from persons in your life?*

They received it! I didn't tell my family for a long time, and my husband said, "OK, just as long as you are working, that's no problem. We'll go to seminary together."

So, I haven't had any resistance. A lot of women have told me about marriages that have broken up due to their call, but my husband and I have been married since December 1972. He's a wonderful husband. We are a neat ministry team.

Additional Comments

I love taking care of my body, and I've been doing that very religiously for most of my life.

I swim and bike (my best friend and I love to bike all the way downtown and back—a ten-mile round trip). I love hiking, running, and walking. I am also a pescatarian.

I absolutely love reading, and I'm in a book club. I love to crochet and knit. I love playing piano and flute. I love singing, preaching, praying, and evangelizing.

I love my family. I have four grandbabies—ages nineteen, ten, four, and two—and I love taking care of them. Yes, I am a very family-oriented person!

Phase 2

1. *Tell the story of your first three years while meeting the requirements necessary for elder's or deacon's ordination or for local pastor's requirements. What were some of your struggles and victories as you pursued answering the call?*

- *Share your stories with the Board(s) of Ordained Ministry. In what ways were they helpful? Did you have any identifiable issues that you were told to improve upon?*
- *If you were assigned to a church(s) during those first three years, what relationships did you have with the parishioners and the community?*
- *When you attended seminary or licensing school, what were your experiences with faculty, staff, and peers? Include the specific years?*

My time with the local licensing school was not difficult. Understandably, seminary was more challenging. District and conference board relationships went well. I was assigned a male mentor, and he was very helpful. He gave encouraging advice and helpful tips on writing the essays. He also gave helpful advice on balancing family, school, ministry, and personal life. I commuted to seminary for two hours for two years, and that was challenging.

The board advised I needed to preach more. I began to fill pulpit supply requests, and I really had a lot of fun expanding in my preaching.

I developed phenomenal relationships at church, and my relationships at home deepened. I became the chaplain for crime victims in my conference.

In seminary, my NT professor and history professor were very instrumental in my professional growth.

2. *Share your stories of each individual appointment since beginning the process for ordination until 2016. Include the following:*

- *What lessons did you learn from each appointment?*
- *What meaningful relationships were established? Include personal, professional, and church member relationships.*
- *What was your personal and church financial state?*
- *Relate any successes or challenges you faced in each appointment. Were there any personal events that affected your ministry (weddings, deaths, or illnesses?)*
- *What Methodist, national, local, or world events affected your appointments? Explain how.*
- *Have any of the meaningful relationships established with your parishioners been continued over the years?*

FIRST APPOINTMENT:
FIRST UMC, ASSOCIATE PASTOR AND CRIME
VICTIM CHAPLAIN, 2005–2009

I was helpful in providing support for crime victims, especially assisting them in survivorship. I formed partnerships and provided training for pastors, agencies, and ministries.

In 2004, I formed a 501(c)(3) nonprofit that provided camp experiences for fifty to seventy-five kids and for parents of murdered children. By 2016, we had 250 campers each summer.

Simultaneously, as associate pastor, I taught Bible study, preached, was involved in the UMW, and officiated at funerals. I was given excellent opportunities to serve and develop my pastoral skills.

Some efforts that required special attention were helping people from different backgrounds work together and keeping people focused on their goals and objectives. Another challenge was being an advocate for persons who didn't know what they needed. I sometimes needed to go to the agency to make a referral for those in need of services.

Meaningful relationships were developed professionally and with partner organizations, especially as we made concerted efforts to maximize our gifts and resources. In addition, great relationships developed within the church. The pastor served as a wonderful mentor to me, and some of the church laity became friends. In fact, one of the members of the UMW became my best friend and is still close to me. Another good friend, an ordained African American pastor, helped me tremendously throughout the candidacy process.

I retired from a job with the federal government, and there was no problem with my finances.

A major event that affected my ministry occurred when my daughter developed a brain malfunction. My daughter had surgery, and the Lord poured out His blessings. After the surgery, my daughter ceased to have seizures. Thanks be to God the professors, pastor, district superintendent and bishop were all supportive. I was in the middle of finals, but God gave me the strength, stamina, and knowledge to pass the tests.

I have always been a health advocate by precept and example. I am an avid exerciser, and I focus on the health and wellness of the whole person.

Meaningful relationships were established at this appointment.

Second Appointment:
Associate pastor, First UMC (cross-cultural appointment), 2009–2012

I was assigned to preaching, Bible study, outreach, visitation, funerals, Sunday school, vacation Bible school, conferences, short-term classes, and administration of discretionary funds.

I learned that if you love people, they will love you back. I attended an Emmaus Walk and developed some very close relationships at that event.

My financial status continued to be good as I received a good salary and benefits.

My preaching was effective in the church. In addition, we went into the community to Central Park for a fun day. There was a good mixture of Black and White people attending. It was an amazing event. Many events were planned that focused on wholeness of mind, body, and spirit. Relationships that had been established when I was chaplain continued.

Third Appointment:
Retirement, 2013–2015

I retired to help my husband with his church, St. Mark UMC (a cross-racial appointment). I was involved in outreach, visitation, and nursing home ministry. I also preached once a month.

Fourth Appointment:
2016, senior pastor, Hawley Memorial and Wesley United Methodist Churches

I preach, administer communion, teach Bible studies, baptize, and serve as chief overseer.

3. Do you see any of your life stories depicted in the lives of the saints in the Bible? Was it helpful to see yourself in scripture as you journeyed in your appointment?

I see myself likened unto Queen Esther. As a person of color, like Esther, I need to be loved, express my voice, and use my gifts. I am grateful to help Caucasian parishioners relate to African American people in Christlike ways, and I have learned much from Caucasian parishioners about the differences in our cultures. My cross-racial appointments have been wonderful learning experiences for all of us.

I see my life depicted in Ruth who had a determination to follow God and go where He sent her. I go where I am sent, and I love all people with boldness and kindness—from the seniors to the children. I love and care for the family of God and the wider community.

4. If you were the first Black woman, or among the firsts, in any of your appointments, state those firsts, and tell the stories. What words of wisdom would you pass on to others who may become pioneers during their ministry?

I was the first African American clergywoman at First UMC in Pine Bluff.

What words of wisdom would you pass on to others who may become pioneers during their ministry?

- Every church needs a great pastor. We become great by loving the people, seeking to understand them, and being patient in developing relationships.
- We should also strive to be open and transparent, explain any concerns, and maintain an open-door policy.
- Things that also worked for me included being accessible, prayerful, loving, and kind.

- I learned the reality of returning good for evil while giving God the glory.
- It is true that we have to meet people where they are and build on that.

5. *In hindsight, how could the annual conference and/or other UM personnel be more helpful when signing Black clergywomen as firsts in a given area of ministry?*

- It would be helpful to require and provide counseling to the Black clergywoman and to key leaders even if they cannot afford counseling. Being left alone without a spiritual female mentor with whom to identify was challenging!
- Denominational leaders should fully support the Black clergywoman in the appointment with phone calls, visits to the church services, and other acts of support.

6. *What personal gifts and graces have been assets to you during your years of ministry? Be specific and relate how they have been helpful.*

- I have the gift of discernment, and with that gift, I am sometimes able to see into the deeper dimensions of the origin of problems. I always pray for discernment to help with decision-making.
- I am an extrovert, and I love people. That helps me to build relationships.
- I am a prayer warrior. I listen to hear from God, and I follow His lead. He always wins the battle.
- My hands-on style of preaching and teaching helps me identify applications of the Bible for life today.
- I embrace diversity, including gender, race, and socioeconomic status, which builds unity in the church.
- I love to provide pastoral care. Visiting the sick and serving them communion is very special to me. It is a time when the

Holy Spirit takes over, and we enter into the holy of holies in a miraculous way.

7. List any particular accomplishments or honors conferred during your years of ministry.

- 2007: Ordained and preached at Annual Conference during a morning session.
- 2007: Jubilee Positive Image Award.
- 2008: First UMC, Crime Victim Advocate of the Year via State of Arkansas.
- 2008–11: Served on the Arkansas Alcohol and Drug Abuse Council for the State of Arkansas.
- 2009–2012: Citizen of Year, Omega Psi Phi Fraternity.
- 2014: Wrote a chapter in *Women Who Lead*.

CHAPTER EIGHT

Bishop Cynthia Moore-Koikoi

Resident Bishop: Pittsburgh Episcopal Area
Conference: Western Pennsylvania
Annual Conference
City: Cranberry Township, Pennsylvania
Age: 51
Year Accepted Call to Ministry: 2000
Year Ordained: 2010

PHASE 1

1. *Recall significant events in your life and society, by decades, beginning with year 1–10, 10–20, etc., until the year you accepted the call to ordained ministry, even if your earlier years were not in a Christian setting. List any songs that were formative in the life events you include in your stories.*

Years 1-10

I was raised in the Methodist church. My father is a United Methodist pastor, now retired, as of Annual Conference 2016. I was actually baptized into the Washington Conference. At that time, we were a segregated church, so it was the all-Black Central Conference within the Methodist Episcopal Church (changed to the United Methodist Church in 1968).

I always enjoyed going to church. I don't know whether or not church was mandatory for us growing up, but I enjoyed it, and the subject never came up. At an early age, I enjoyed being involved in Sunday school and those kinds of things.

Years 10-20

I accepted Jesus Christ as my personal Savior when I was twelve years old at a youth retreat. Every year, the youth from the Baltimore-Washington Conference would go to the "Youth Assembly." At this particular Youth Assembly, we had communion, and after communion, the celebrant said, "Go out and find a spot—and just spend some time talking with God."

That kind of contemplative, meditative prayer was new to me, but being an obedient child who loved church, I thought, *Okay, I'm going to go out here and find some place on this mountain.* In the midst of my praying, I started to cry. I didn't know why I was crying, but I couldn't stop. During that emotional time, I heard what sounded to me like an audible voice from God: "You are a good girl, Cynthia, but you've got to get this for yourself. It's not good enough that your great-grandparents knew me, and it's not good enough that your grandparents or your parents knew me. You have to know me for yourself."

In that moment, I recalled some turmoil I was having with my mom at the time—typical issues for a growing twelve-year-old. I had some arguments with my mom, and the guilt and the weight of that came to mind. However, almost immediately, there was a release and a feeling of forgiveness from that guilt. I said, "Jesus, I'm yours. I'm yours." I started a more personal relationship from that time on. Until that time, it had been a more intellectual relationship—as intellectual as you can get at that age—but from that moment, it became more of a spiritual and emotional connection and growth with God.

Through my high school years, I continued to be very active in the church, assuming leadership roles in the church while being nurtured by my parents, but I was not required by my parents to do those types of things. I wanted to be a part of the leadership in our youth group and participate in various church activities.

In the midst of doing those things, people in the church were saying, "You know, I think you have a call. You are going to follow in your dad's footsteps." At that point, it did not seem even remotely possible. Being a pastor was not something I felt called to do, but I do remember having those conversations.

YEARS 20-30

After college, I moved to Baltimore and attended a couple of churches. I took on a leadership role in the church. I became a certified lay speaker (as we called them at that point and time in history). I also served as worship leader and youth coordinator and in various other offices in the church. I was particularly supported by the pastor at Sharp Street when I joined there. He also gave me opportunities to preach, teach, and form the worship experiences that we had at Sharp Street.

It wasn't until 2000 that I eventually surrendered to my call.

List any songs that were formative in the life events you include in your stories.

One of the songs that mean a lot to me asks, "Were you there?" It's hard for me to sing that song without coming to tears, partly because

I remember singing that song when my mom was in the hospital. During my adolescent years, she was having a routine appendectomy. I remember feeling a connection to her and feeling concerned about her while she was in the hospital. God was ministering to me through that hymn.

The other song that really had an impact on me was "Pass It On." That was a song we sang a lot at the different youth gatherings in the Baltimore-Washington Conferences as I was growing up. We would sing that song with gusto. In fact, we were singing that song during the celebration of communion when I received that warming of my heart that John Wesley talked about. It was an assurance of my salvation.

Those two songs, in particular, were very formative in my growing up, and they were very formative in my acceptance of Jesus Christ as my Lord and Savior.

2. Recall the people who significantly contributed to your Christian formation up to the acceptance of the call. Tell the stories of how they influenced your life.

My parents—and my father in particular—were very instrumental in my Christian formation. I am clearly a "daddy's girl," and I always have been. I spent a lot of time with my dad. My dad's the kind of person who, in raising us, would engage in conversation, and we would talk about the great questions of the world.

I remember a conversation when I was in elementary school. We had this coffee table that was a glass enclosure, and inside of the glass enclosure was a train layout with a whole town that my dad had made. My dad said, "So, I wonder if we are like this layout. Perhaps, we are in God's eyesight, and He is picturing us in this layout." That led to this wonderful conversation about who God is and about His existence. I was probably in fourth or fifth grade, but we had a great conversation. We continued to have those types of conversations throughout the years.

Shortly after my conversion experience, I was at a youth event, and the youth coordinator was driving my sister and me home when we had a car accident. I remember feeling like we were in slow motion as I saw the car approaching a tree, and we crashed into it. We got out of the car, and a man said, "Praise God that God was with you." Then he disappeared. I don't know where he went. Later, as I was talking to my dad, I said, "You know, I was praying before this accident that I wanted to get back to that fervor that I had at my conversion experience, and I am wondering whether or not God did this so that I could get back to that place."

My father said, "No that's not how God works. God does not need to use tragedy for those kinds of things. There are natural ebbs and flows in our relationship with God. There are times when we feel really close, and there are times when we feel really distant; they are just part of the Christian journey." Even though my dad didn't use the terminology, I found out later on he was talking about the "dark night of the soul." My dad has been a really important and significant part of my Christian formation.

According to my siblings, my mother and I are very much alike. There were times when I had to repent for those adolescent years. I was a very respectful child. I'm not talking about yelling or screaming or anything like that, but I had some disagreements with my mother about the coat that I should buy or the money to buy jeans. She thought young ladies shouldn't wear jeans. I needed to repent for those arguments. Mother patiently worked with me through those things and offered forgiveness. In addition, I would see her model being a lady. When my dad was actively serving, she was doing things like hosting committee meetings in the parsonage, working with the United Methodist Women, and occasionally teaching. My mom was not one to be in front of anybody, but she was always supportive and doing things behind the scenes.

I'm the kind of leader who enjoys getting my hands dirty as I lead, and I get that from my mom because she was always working at the church and getting her hands dirty. She'd be there on Saturday mornings. When we were going to have some type of dinner after church, she'd be there peeling the potatoes. That's the kind of leadership that I enjoy, and that feeds me when I am able to do those kinds of servant-leadership things. My mom influenced me by showing me how to be a good servant and leader.

My paternal grandparents influenced me, especially with their prayers. My father's mother had some significant health concerns. She was diabetic and a double amputee. There were sometimes that she was in great pain, and I could hear her calling out lovingly to Jesus while she was in the pain. She asked Jesus to heal her and help her. Those prayers had a profound impact on me.

All four grandparents had a relationship with Jesus Christ, and their homes were built upon solid Christian foundations. That was formative for me. They really set good examples and were role models for me. My mom and dad were poised to teach and raise their children in the love and admonition of Jesus Christ and to personify a walk with Christ.

A member of Sharp Street was particularly instrumental in my acceptance of my call. On a Sunday, after I had preached, I was receiving people at the back of the sanctuary. The member said, "You know that you are called to the ministry. You know that?"

I said, "No, I don't know that."

She said, "Well, God told me—so I'm telling you."

I said, "Well, God hasn't told me yet."

She said, "Thank you, now I know exactly how to pray."

I thought, *Okay, it's all over now, Cynthia! I won't be able to run anymore.*

That member was a prayer warrior like no other! I knew it was all over then, and it was! A series of things kept happening, so I couldn't resist my call anymore.

One of those important conversations I had was with a pastor who was a friend of my dad's. I was away at a BMCR meeting, and he and I just happened to sit at the same table for lunch. We were talking about all different kinds of things, and he said, "So, why are you reluctant to accept your call?"

I said, "We weren't talking about a call. I don't have a call."

He said, "Yes, you do—and I know that you have been thinking about it. What is your reluctance?"

Again, somebody had been talking or speaking to him! That somebody was some angelic or spiritual force that was speaking to him. We talked about it, and I know that one of the questions was the reason for my reluctance to the call. Part of what I shared with him was at that point, I was making good money as a school psychologist. I didn't know if I could give up that to go into ministry.

My first job as a school psychologist paid me more money than my dad was making, and by that point, he had about thirty years of experience as a full-time clergyperson. I said, "So, that is a real concern for me because I like nice things." We talked that through, and I also said, "I don't know any good role models of married women in ministry." All the women in ministry who I knew were single—at least those who were doing it well. I had secretly prayed to God: "If you find me a man, then I'll answer my call." I believed I would need a man who would be willing to accept that part of who I am. So, two things were really a deterrent for me accepting my call: not having positive married role models and the financial thing.

Dad's friend talked me through that and got me to a place where I was at least open to consider having a conversation with God. I really hadn't talked to God about it yet. I knew that other people were talking about it, but I hadn't yet opened myself up to say, "God, what do you want to say to me?"

3. *Recall the people/events that significantly served to deter your affirming the call to ordained ministry.*

On a Sunday, the pastor of Sharp Street Church announced to the congregation that I had accepted my call to ministry.

In the process of greeting people in the back of the church, one of the dear saints of the church, an older gentleman, said, "I'm so happy because I believe that you are called by God, but I hope that the bishop never sends you here."

I said, "What do you mean?"

He said, "I don't want to have a woman minister." He was personally affirming my call, but he was not able to see the vision of being led by a woman. He was somebody I loved very deeply and a fine Christian figure in the church. His words were not a deterrent, but they were certainly not an encouragement.

I was working as a school psychologist at the time of my call, and the faculty and staff had formed a prayer group (with the permission of the principal.) Some of us would gather before school and pray for the day, pray for the students, and for other things.

A gentleman at the school heard that I had accepted my call to ministry and walked me to my car. He said, "You need to shake that thing! That's from the devil! Women aren't called to ministry." I had to close my car door on him. That was a scary thing.

I thought, *What am I going to be up against? What am I going to have to face as a female clergyperson? Will I be in places where I feel physically threatened?* That was kind of a deterrent, and if I hadn't been sure at that time that I was called by God, that could have deterred me. I praise the Lord for the grounding before that happened!

Another potential deterrent was my first husband. He and I actually went through spiritual counseling because he had a Catholic background—and then he was nondenominational—and he didn't really have a concept of a woman being in a lead position in the church. Fortunately, when we got engaged, he was worshipping at a Baptist church that believed in the ordination of women. We did some counseling with his pastor, and he directed him to some other male spouses of ordained clergywomen. We spent some time talking through and exploring that. We got married, but it ultimately ended in divorce. That could have been a deterrent, but by the grace of God, I was strong enough in the Lord to continue on without my husband.

4. *When you received the call to ordained ministry, did you respond yes immediately and take appropriate action? Why or why not?*

I have to answer yes and no to that question. Before I answered yes, I knew. However, I had put up so many excuses and barriers to the call that it wasn't okay for me to say no. I could endure saying no, but there came a point when I could not endure it anymore. When I got to that point, I said yes—and it was all green lights from there.

I told my pastor and my parents, and I looked into enrolling into seminary immediately at that point. I didn't look back after that.

5. *What was your occupation when you received the call, and what effect did it have on your response?*

I was a school psychologist when I received my call, and I was blessed to be working with a lot of folks who were Christians. The principal and the vice principal were Christian folks who were really involved in their church. They were not just pew sitters, and they were able to celebrate with me. My supervisor was a Jewish woman, but she was very much a woman of faith. She was also able to celebrate my call with me, and she assisted in the transition.

Although the school didn't have a practice of allowing psychologists to be part-time, she allowed me to be part-time so that I could take classes and serve a church while I was still a school psychologist. Things fell into line there. Having that support from the people I was working with really helped me make that transition and answer the call.

Having a background in psychology helped me answer the call, and it helped me immensely in those early stages of my ministry. I was going to school and was hired at a large church for a while. When I first started out, I was working to help set up their pastoral counseling program. Later, I was appointed to serve a small church. I was doing the same things and using the same skill sets in my church jobs and in my secular job, which helped make it a smooth transition from the secular to the more sacred.

6. *If you did not take immediate action to the call, recall the thinking/ rationale that caused resistance to your immediate response.*

Some of the things I have already articulated as to my rationale, including the lack of married women role models and needing to work on trusting God for my finances.

I'll tell you a story about the financial resistance. As I was wrestling with the financial issue, I happened to go to an event at Cokesbury Bookstore.

The person who was checking me out said, "You look like you could use the clergy discount."

I said, "I didn't realize there was a clergy discount." I realized God was saying, "See? I've got this all worked out! You are worried about the financial end of it, but I've got this all worked out!"

God dealt with my resistance all along the way. I talked about having to work through what it would look like to be married and be in ministry. There was something else that had escaped my mind. My father and I have different personalities. My father is a shepherd by disposition. He is very calm and peaceful. He is always about reconciliation, shepherding, and caring for the flock, and he has endless patience. At the time of my call, that was not me! I was very impatient. I did not see myself as a shepherd, and I felt uncomfortable with hospital visits even though I did them. Even as a layperson, when I went with the pastor and others to do hospital visits and helped serve communion and those types of things, I just felt uncomfortable. I did not like preaching at all. Even though the pastor gave me a lot of opportunities to do it, it always felt like a chore to me.

I prayed to God and said, "I'm not at all like my dad. I don't have his disposition! I don't think I would be a good pastor!"

I had a dream about a really high pulpit. I felt something pulling me to the pulpit. I was resisting that pull, and I said, "That's my dad's pulpit! I'm not fit for that!"

The resistance said, "No, that's your pulpit!"

I had some more conversations with God about that, and He reassured me that He had called me out of who I was—and not out of who my dad was. During that time, the first Black clergywoman had just been elected bishop in the AME Church, and she came to preach the ordination service for the United Methodist Baltimore/ Washington Annual Conference. During her sermon, she was speaking directly to the female ordinands, and she said, "God called you just as you are—the woman! Don't try to cover up or hide the fact that you are a woman. God made you to be uniquely who you are in the service of God's church."

That was a freeing moment. Yes, God had called my dad to the ministry, but now God was calling me—somebody different—to the ministry because that's what God needed at that time. That's also one of the reasons why I usually preach in heels. I like to remind myself that God called me as a woman. Not all women wear heels, but for me, one of the signs of my femininity is my heels. I inherited that from my great-grandmother. She wore heels all the time until she couldn't walk anymore, and for me, that is a sign that God called me in all of my womanhood to ministry.

7. *What occurred that enabled you to overcome the resistance to answering the call?*

A vision enabled me to move beyond my resistance to the call. I think it was because of the prayers, meditations, and mystical experiences I had during those times. I wrote a paper in seminary about how women have mystical experiences to affirm their calls. There is something about our makeup that God speaks to and works with us through those mystical experiences. Something about the mystique of those mystical experiences helps keep us stay grounded when we undergo the resistance, the distractions, and those who say, "No, you can't be a pastor."

Yes. It's the vision, and if you look throughout history, most women who have been called in the church had those visions. They've had mystical experiences that have helped keep them grounded.

8. *What was the time frame between receiving the call and saying yes with appropriate action?*

If I marked the beginning, it would be about two years. If I marked the point where I said okay, it was a couple of years before I let my pastor know.

9. What role did the church play in your answering or not answering the call immediately?

The church played a role in helping me answer the call more immediately. A woman said the Lord told her He was calling me into the ministry.

Other folks said, "You're called. I can see it."

My dad's friend at the BMCR meeting asked me prompting and probing questions. These encounters played a significant role in positively answering the call.

Some folks, even though they didn't articulate it until after the pastor had announced my call, showed by their actions that they were not particularly affirming of women in ministry. Not answering the call was also reinforced by the lack of positive female married role models and seeing that female pastors were not treated as kindly.

10. Were there any spiritual disciplines that played a role in your resistance or acceptance of the call? Tell the stories.

Definitely! Prayer, meditation, asking God for guidance, and the incidents that happened after particularly intense prayers, my dream, the conversation at Cokesbury, and the conversation with the friend of my dad all came after times of intense prayer and meditation.

I hadn't been fasting in those years, but during the time of my call, I had a practice of fasting. A couple of times, I did a weeklong fast for discernment. That was the time I kind of knew that I was called, but I still had barriers to answering the call. I would go away for a week at a time, do a weeklong fast, and pray for discernment. Those times were very special to me. They were times of real connection with God, connection with myself, connection with my body, and connection with nature. Yes, the fasting was very helpful.

11. In retrospect, how do you see God's hand at work in your life that prepared you for ordained ministry?

Growing up in the church and being under the tutelage of an excellent pastor—my father—prepared me. Actually, I feel absolutely grounded in Christian foundations and in having a good church family. My dad has served wonderful churches, and I had the excellent Sunday school teachers. I worked with good folks in the youth group, and faithful mentors taught me.

I had the good grounding of saints. At a very early age, one of those saints was a member of the church where my dad served when I was born (Asbury in Shepherd's Town). I was just two years old when we left that church, but one of the members of that church said, "I'm going to be at Cynthia's graduation when she graduates from high school." That gentleman kept in touch with me and our family, and sure enough, at my graduation from high school, he was sitting right there.

At the annual conference, I was endorsed to run for bishop. The church choir from Asbury in Shepherd's Town was invited to sing at one of the worship services, and that gentleman was still in the choir. He embraced me and sent me off with a blessing for the process of becoming a bishop. This gentleman followed me through high school, and he was still with me when I became bishop. That's the church! That's the church!

I have been supported and undergirded by prayers from people like the Asbury gentleman in the church, and that's God working and preparing me for ordained ministry.

I had my mom, dad, and the church family. My dad was an excellent pastoral role model, my mom taught and encouraged me in hands-on leadership skills, and the church family surrounded me with love, care, and guidance. I think God was working through all these people to prepare me for ordained ministry.

God was preparing me for ministry as He led me to the profession of school psychology. When I started as an undergrad, I didn't know anything about school psychology. I knew about psychology, and I knew about education—but I didn't know there was such a field as school psychology. By happenstance, I was walking through a job fair, and I saw somebody who was a school psychologist and started a conversation with him. The preparation that I got in organizational psychology and abnormal psychology helped me with ordained ministry. God also placed me in a secular work environment where I was surrounded by people of faith, which doesn't often happen in government organizations. I was surrounded by people of faith while working in a public school system.

God gave me a supervisor who understood the call. Even though she was not Christian, but a member of the Jewish faith, she understood and was willing to work with me and prepare me. Having a principal who allowed me to have prayer meetings and all those kinds of things, that was God! That absolutely was God!

12. *When you accepted the call to ministry, what was the response from persons in your life?"*

All of my siblings have been very supportive, and they were supportive from the beginning. My sister, in particular, stated from the beginning that she knew already that I had a call, but she didn't mention it until I acknowledged my call.

Yes, many people said, "Yeah, we knew it was about time." That was kind of the response. That was an affirmation! My close friends all said, "We believe you are called, and we will support you in whatever ways we can."

My church family was affirming—except for the one gentleman who did not want me to pastor his church. Ironically, he still supported me in my call. Folks assured me that they would help in whatever ways I needed help. They helped me with the process of seminary, with whatever recommendations I needed, and in other ways. My church family was just great.

PHASE 2

1. *Tell the story of your first three years while meeting the requirements necessary for elder's or deacon's ordination or for local pastor's*

requirements. What were some of your struggles and victories as you pursued answering the call?

- *Share your stories with the Board(s) of Ordained Ministry. In what ways were they helpful? Did you have any identifiable issues that you were told to improve upon?*
- *If you were assigned to a church(s) during those first three years, what relationships did you have with the parishioners and the community?*
- *When you attended seminary or licensing school, what were your experiences with faculty, staff, and peers? Include the specific years?*

I began attending Wesley Theological Seminary part-time while working full-time as a school psychologist. I was assigned to an ecumenical congregation as a student pastor. It was an independent former AME church with staff from other denominations. I served there for a couple years. I experienced a struggle trying to balance working full-time as a school psychologist, part-time at the church, and part-time at the seminary.

I started as a part-time student at Wesley Seminary, and when my job changed to part-time, I was able to become a full-time student. I joined diverse prayer groups that met weekly. A few of the groups included Bible study, but most were mainly prayer groups.

I intentionally chose the most conservative professors, the opposite of me, to enhance my education. My church leadership class was taught by a Baptist professor who didn't believe in women in key leadership roles. I knew that it would be a challenge. He would make highly conservative remarks stating that women should teach only women and children. We disagreed amicably.

At Wesley, there was a mandatory requirement to take a class at one of the seminaries in the consortium that Wesley was a member of. I took a class in church leadership and enjoyed the class greatly. The professor was fair in the grading process.

I started the seminary in 2000 and graduated in 2010.

The Board of Ordained Ministry was helpful and assigned me to an excellent elder for a mentor. I considered it a "God pairing." He was strong in my area of weakness, which was administrative. My gift was pastoral care. Also, he was sensitive to my life situation.

I was married and then divorced. My first husband had difficulty adjusting to being married to a woman pastor. My mentor helped as he shared personal struggles that he, other clergy, and spouses had worked through. The ordination process was fairly smooth. I received support as needed. We had a good group mentor who was helpful in preparing us for ordination exams.

After serving approximately three years in the ecumenical church, the mentor said the district needed and wanted me in a UM church. I received a couple of offers. The first was in East Baltimore at a Caucasian church, formerly an Evangelical United Brethren, where the neighborhood was in transition. The church began outreach to the transitioning Hispanic population, and I was involved in most of the outreach. I conducted Bible studies on the stoop of the church-owned house and other venues.

2. Share your stories of each individual appointment since beginning the process for ordination until 2016. Include the following:

- *What lessons did you learn from each appointment?*
- *What meaningful relationships were established? Include personal, professional, and church member relationships.*
- *What was your personal and church financial state?*
- *Relate any successes or challenges you faced in each appointment. Were there any personal events that affected your ministry (weddings, deaths, or illnesses?)*
- *What Methodist, national, local, or world events affected your appointment? Explain How.*
- *Have any of the meaningful relationships established with your parishioners been continued over the years?*

FIRST APPOINTMENT:
STUDENT PASTOR, 2004–2007

In my first appointment, I was a student pastor in East Baltimore from 2004 until 2007. I learned that people are afraid and anxious when they see their church shrinking (decreasing in membership and/or finances). As a pastor, I was able to express hope and point out different experiences that were helpful.

The church was in a transitional neighborhood, and the church was not connected. In fact, White flight from the city impacted the church. I was able to establish a good relationship with the lay leader, and we were able to help the church move forward.

The financial state of the church was horrendous. I was the first part-time pastor. The previous pastor was full-time with the assistance of "equitable salary funds." I received five overdue bills my first day. The debt was overwhelming, and in six months, the boiler exploded. We reached out to previous members, near and far, and the response was extraordinary. We abundantly received more than was needed. The appeal was a success.

There were no national events that affected the ministry.

SECOND APPOINTMENT:
ASSOCIATE PASTOR, 2007–2010

In my second appointment, I served as the associate pastor from 2007 until 2010 in Annapolis, Maryland. I was able to utilize and expand my administrative skills. I learned how to implement and administer policy and procedures in a large-membership church. I learned additional lessons in getting the leadership behind you. The church didn't have a voucher system in place, but I designed and implemented one that became standard operational procedure.

While I was there, I began to interact with a Black ecumenical group, and I realized I needed to develop good relationships with churches other than the one I was serving. We had good conversations on racism in the churches, and I was able to further cultivate skills in race relations. I also became aware of how the majority White congregation impacted the impressions in the community.

I started a women's Bible study, and it exploded, resulting in three Bible studies. I used the text written by Bishop Vashti McKenzie of the AME denomination. The Bible study was not just for Methodists; it was for the community.

The finances of the church were wonderful and undergirded with an endowment of one million dollars. The committee would award twenty-five thousand per year to missions after determining which local, national, and international missions would receive awards.

I was paid well and had no financial struggles. While I was in seminary, my tuition and fees were paid by the Ministerial Education Fund, Georgia Harkness Scholarship, and Douglas Memorial Community Church in Baltimore. I graduated debt-free.

Challenges developed due to differences in race and culture. I was serving a White congregation with a different worship style than I was accustomed to. They had contemporary and traditional styles of worship as was common in a White church. Consequently, I sought to attend services where the worship style was more charismatic or apostolic. There were political differences as well. I preached that health care was a right and not a privilege, and I got a lot of pushback.

I experienced successes in Bible study classes, and ecumenical relations. In addition, I was able to facilitate a service to help bridge the congregations' racial divide by having an MLK Jr. service at the White church with a Black congregation attending.

Personal challenges evolved around getting divorced and entering my second marriage. I was concerned how the congregation would respond, but I was pleasantly surprised when they were supportive of me.

A national event that affected the church was the election of President Obama, which resulted in a greater Republican/Democratic divide. Some church members were for Obama, and some were against him. Intensive work was needed to encourage the congregation to be welcoming to all, regardless.

The relationships that evolved from that ministry were phenomenal. Some of us still are in contact through Facebook and times of prayer. A woman and her husband helped me discern to run for bishop. The husband didn't believe in women pastors, but he grew and asked me to baptize his grandchild. In fact, I contacted that couple and utilized their story in preparation for the annual conference to endorse me as a candidate for bishop.

Third Appointment:
discipler guide, 2010–2012

My third appointment was as a discipler guide. I served in that position from 2010 until 2012. I worked under two district superintendents by assisting them, presiding over church conferences, and helping churches with their finances. I became good friends with the district superintendents.

I was in a different learning mode for administration at that level in the church. I also became aware of spiritual things about some of my colleagues that were troubling, and that was a challenge. I observed acceleration in closure of churches in the United Methodist denomination along with the need to discern whether or not to close or look at other transition options.

I was paid well, and I encountered no financial difficulties.

I developed good friendships with a few people, including secretaries, and we still keep contact through phone calls, texts, and dinners and luncheons.

Fourth Appointment:
district superintendent, Greater Washington District

In my fourth appointment, from 2012 until 2013, I served as district superintendent of the Greater Washington District.

FIFTH APPOINTMENT:
DISTRICT SUPERINTENDENT, 2013–2016

I was appointed as district superintendent of the Baltimore Metropolitan District from 2013 until 2016.

My relationships continued with the two district superintendents I had previously served with in my previous appointment. In addition, a second bishop (mentor) helped me discern the call to submit my name for nomination as bishop. I was then married to my present husband who was fully supportive. He was also processing as a clergyperson. His family also embraced me.

I faced several challenges as district superintendent. One challenge was not having enough time for all the duties. Another challenge was a Black clergywoman who was not encouraging, but I intentionally sought to develop a relationship with her. My efforts resulted in a friendship, and she later became very supportive.

Other challenges included downsizing of churches and addressing delinquent pension and medical payments in some churches. We developed a plan to address this with much success. We were able to assist several churches in increasing their budgets, which led to greater stability

During my time as district superintendent, Freddie Gray was killed by police officers, which was followed by community unrest. I gave leadership in assisting our churches to reach out to the community. Children were accepted into the churches while school was closed. Food donations and supplies that were needed by families were distributed. Despite the tragedy, the churches and community groups worked together.

Relationships were harder to cultivate as a district superintendent. However, some have maintained contact and welcomed me as bishop.

SIXTH ASSIGNMENT:
ELECTION AS BISHOP IN THE NORTHEASTERN JURISDICTION, 2016

I was assigned to the Western Pennsylvania Conference in 2016.

3. Do you see any of your life stories depicted in the lives of the saints in the Bible? Was it helpful to see yourself in scripture as you journeyed in your appointment?

I relate to the Psalm 139 because it is very helpful when things are tough or when I need encouragement. It is helpful for me to remember that "I am fearfully and wonderfully made." It is empowering to know that God made provision for the calling on my life while I was in the womb.

I see similarities in Judge Deborah. One of my roles as bishop is to judge with wisdom. At times, I affirm people in their calls while enabling and empowering them.

I see my life depicted in Mary, the mother of Jesus, who "pondered in her heart." In the process of pondering, I get inspiration. In some decisions, timing is very important. Sometimes I need to work things out in my heart and then share them—so I don't sabotage what God is doing.

4. If you were the first Black woman, or among the firsts, in any of your appointments, state those firsts, and tell the stories. What words of wisdom would you pass on to others who may become pioneers during their ministry?

- I was the first African American clergywoman assigned to the church in Annapolis. There was some resistance to women in ministry and theological differences.
- I was among the first female discipler guides, but it was not such a big deal because there were already some district superintendents who were women of color.
- I was the first African American clergywoman assigned as bishop of the Western Pennsylvania Conference.

What words of wisdom would you pass on to others who may become pioneers during their ministry?

- Embrace Black womanhood—and don't try to be anything else. A female bishop in the AME church encouraged me to lead as a woman and as a Black woman.
- Have a close Black female confidante to share your life and hold you accountable.
- Be attentive to self-care.
- Establish boundaries.
- Don't sweat every complaint.
- Do not get wrapped up in other people's agendas.
- Be proactive and stay connected.
- Don't respond to every little offense.
- A district superintendent said, "You don't have to prove that you are a district superintendent, pastor, etcetera." Leading with that knowledge has been of tremendous help as I have continued to be a pioneer in many ways.

5. *In hindsight, how could the annual conference and/or other UM personnel be more helpful when signing Black clergywomen as firsts in a given area of ministry?*

- Do more prep work with the congregation and the Black clergywoman to be assigned.
- Uncover unconscious stuff going on by having a series of meetings—not just one.
- African American clergywomen need to know that the bishop and cabinet have their backs by being supportive, especially when conflicts arise.
- Utilize services and resources of the General Commission on Religion and Race.

6. *What personal gifts and graces have been assets to you during your years of ministry? Be specific and relate how they have been helpful?*

- I am an active listener. The skills I acquired as a school psychologist became very useful as I served as pastor, district superintendent, and bishop. I listen to people's anxieties and fears, and I want them to know they have been heard.

- Administration is now one of my strong points, but I was weak in administration when I started in the ministry. Mentors have helped me along the way, and I am now strong in that area.
- I am madly in love with "process." For everything we do, I insist on a procedural manual and/or organizational structure. This leads to more efficiency in making disciples.
- I try to build bridges. I try to make people comfortable. I value their opinions, and I hear their voices. This is helpful in Western Pennsylvania when there is racism or when churches say, "We don't want a female pastor." A woman hugged me and said, "I am racist, and I love you!" I realized in that moment that I needed to build a bridge—even to her.

7. *List any particular accomplishments or honors conferred during your years of ministry.*

- Mayor's citation for service to the community in the city of Baltimore.
- Recognition as one of the "Top Black Women in Pittsburgh" by the *Pittsburgh-Post Gazette*.
- District superintendent of Greater Washington District.
- District superintendent of Baltimore Metropolitan District.
- Elected bishop in the Northeastern Jurisdiction.
- Assigned as the first African American female bishop in Western Pennsylvania.

CHAPTER NINE

Rev. Ella H. DeDeaux

Churches: St. Paul UMC, Pass
Christian, Mississippi, and Mt. Zion
UMC, DeLisle, Mississippi
Conference: Mississippi
Age: 63
Year accepted the call to ministry: 2008
Year Ordained: 2016

PHASE 1

1. Recall significant events in your life and society, by decades, beginning with year 1–10, 10–20, etc., until the year you accepted the call to ordained ministry, even if your earlier years were not in a Christian setting. List any songs that were formative in the life events you include in your stories.

YEARS 1–10

As a child, my parents taught me about God and how to rely on Jesus Christ as my Lord and Savior. I was brought to church before I could talk or walk. I went to Sunday school, eleven o'clock service, Baptist Training Union (BTU), and night service. I was taught the books of the Bible during Monday's prayer band time. During this time of church attendance, I found myself in church more than I wanted to be. At the age of five, I joined church and was baptized. After baptism, I sang in the sunshine choir and was a junior usher. My parents played an important role in my formative years as a Christian.

YEARS 10–20

As a teenager, I progressed to the junior choir and began to participate in teen activities. My siblings and I represented our church as delegates in the Fifth Sunday Congress and other district pageants.

I entered college at the age of sixteen with the idea that I would not live past the age of thirty-five. In college, I rarely attended church unless I went home for the holidays. However, when I faced trials in college, I would go to the chapel at night to pray and sing "Precious Lord, Take My Hand." Little did I know the foundation my parents laid for me would be utilized by my minute faith. In using this small faith, I began to depend on God for myself.

YEARS 20–30

After finishing college, I returned home and started to develop a relationship with God. This relationship was still more one-sided than it should have been. I was very much on the receiving side of the relationship and not on the side of giving more of my life to Christ. During this time in my life, I was already a divorced single parent. I attended church so my eldest son would have the same foundation that was afforded me by my parents. I became very active, including singing in the adult choir, starting a youth group, teaching Sunday school, and speaking for several women's events at the church. I also attended other local churches.

Years 30-40

After several years of being a single mother, I prayed for a husband to help raise my son. I was also reflecting on the idea that I wouldn't live past thirty-five, which was shortly around the corner. Because I was impatient, I moved in my own will and married a longtime friend in 1981. This marriage lasted three years. As I look back, I was not ready for marriage because I didn't have an understanding of what a godly wife was. I was only pretending.

My relationship with Christ was not there. I was only pretending in front of friends, family, church, and God. I worked in the church, and if others were asked about my Christian walk, the answer would have been a profound, implicit, and enthusiastic "model strong Christian," but I was a pretender. By this time, I was now a two-time divorcee with two children—and thirty-five was speedily approaching.

Nearing age thirty-five, and becoming anxious about my spiritual life, I began to realize the need to stop pretending and strengthen this relationship I professed to have with God. The first thing I realized was that I must open myself up and give God more control of my life. I had to learn how to use the faith I had. I continued to work in church, and it gradually became less and less about me and more and more about the God in me. God worked with me to the point where I could trust the faith I had in Him.

I was directed by God to move to Fort Collins, Colorado. This was a leap of faith because I didn't know anyone there, and I had no prospect of a job and no place to stay. My thought was that I was going to continue my education, but little did I know that God was beginning to make me a new creature. My family reluctantly helped me pack up my house and load a Budget rental truck. My eldest son and I drove from Pass Christian, Mississippi, to Fort Collins.

The very first thing I learned when we arrived in Fort Collins was that we needed to pray together as a family. We had to get direction from God about what our next steps would be. The first order of business was finding a place to stay. The continued hotel stay was eating into the funds we needed to move into a permanent place.

Moving to a college town and finding a place to stay in August was more difficult than I had imagined it would be. We continued to pray as a family each night and morning as we looked for an apartment. We found a duplex in the foothills within a week. God is faithful in His promises and loving toward all He has made.

Next was finding a job. I went on four interviews: two at the administration office and two with principals. God allows us the opportunity to glorify His name at the most peculiar times. During my second interview, I let the principal know that God had brought me to Fort Collins and that He had a job for me in Fort Collins. If I doubted God's faithfulness before, He showed me what's for me is for me. The principal had temporarily hired someone for the fourth-grade teaching position, but the person was unable to pass the required test to teach in Colorado. Instead, I was hired. God was showing favor to my children and me—just as He has done for so many people in the Bible.

2. Recall the people who significantly contributed to your Christian Formation up to the acceptance of the call. Tell the stories of how they influenced your life.

After two years of teaching in Colorado, I found myself being RIFed (reduction in force) from my job. I was without a job, and unemployment barely covered my rent. I was on food stamps. It was September. I was searching for a job, and I was solely dependent on God for my source while reading the psalms and praying.

One of my friends asked me to spend a weekend at Estes Park, Colorado, at something called Koinonia. I found a babysitter and attended an unforgettable and life-changing experience. This was the first of many Koinonia experiences that broadened my understanding of God Almighty and the meaning of Jesus's love. The statement that God is no respecter of person, in Romans 2:11, was brought to mind as I was able to experience Caucasians truly displaying God's unconditional love. My prior experiences in Mississippi had never revealed this to be the case.

As my life and belief of Christianity were changing and growing, I also saw the lives of others doing likewise. I began to understand Jesus as the ultimate love example. While trusting in God's promises, I started teaching in October when another teacher took a sabbatical. After a year, I had the opportunity to participate on a Koinonia team as a speaker. I was in prayer that the Holy Spirit would speak through me as I worked on the subject of piety for several weeks. I was planning to only reveal a small portion of myself to the group. When I went to the podium, I had a friend pray with and over me. As I began to say what I had rehearsed, the Holy Spirit took over and opened my mouth to reveal the part of me He desired and what the group needed to hear. When I finished, I realized my prayers had been answered and that Christ had spoken through me in a powerful way.

My mother died while I still lived in Colorado, and I decided to move back to Mississippi in 1997. My daughter was graduating from high school in the spring of 1998. I was beginning to feel the emotional drain due to the losses of my parents and brother while I lived in Colorado. I realized that the death I spoke of at age fifteen was a spiritual death.

Upon returning to Mississippi, I joined Mt. Zion United Methodist Church, and I continued my spiritual growth. I became very active in Mt. Zion UMC, becoming the church financial secretary, volunteering in the church office, working with the children, starting a food program for low-income families in the community, and working with youth ministries, children's sermons, and as treasurer—though not all at the same time. For six years, I attended lay speaker, discipleship, stewardship, and "Strengthening the Black Church for the Twenty-First Century" training.

3. Recall the people/events that significantly served to deter your affirming the call to ordained ministry.

The year 2005 came in like a roller coaster. My only daughter, at age twenty-four, was shot and killed in New Orleans on February 1. She was planning my wedding, and there was a void that only God could fill. We decided to continue with the wedding, and I was married on June 25, 2005. This date is significant because Hurricane Katrina hit two months later. We lost everything. The hardest and most difficult part of Katrina was the loss of all my daughter's pictures. The year was not over yet. My stepdaughter was married in December. This hit me very hard because I realized my daughter would never experience marriage or children. My health was also failing, and I had to have surgery in December. The only thing that sustained me during 2005 was the grace of God.

The following year, I attended "Winds of the Spirit," a healing seminar. I knew that God was calling me to something more, and I began to ask for direction and clarity to do His will.

I was unaware of the anger I held toward God for the murder of my daughter. During one of the discussions and prayers, I realized God could not take me any further in my spiritual growth until I released the anger. I began to be unhappy teaching, which was very unusual because I had a passion for teaching. I knew that one of the gifts that God had blessed me with was the ability and the desire to teach. My husband and I were still living in a FEMA recreational vehicle, and God was strengthening me individually and in the unity of my marriage.

4. *When you received the call to ordained ministry, did you respond yes immediately and take appropriate action? Why or why not?*

I quit my job in 2007 and began discerning my call by praying, reading scripture, and fasting as a way to open myself to God. It took a year, but during a Katrina remembrance service in 2008, God revealed my call to the ministry. I spoke with my husband and my pastor, and they both encouraged me in this new step of my life. However, I felt some resistance to the call and could not identify why.

5. *What was your occupation when you received the call, and what effect did it have on your response?*

I had quit my job to discern my call, and I did not have an active occupation when I received the call to ministry.

6. If you did not take immediate action to the call, recall the thinking/ rationale that caused resistance to your immediate response.

I spent two years discerning my call through prayer, fasting, meditation, tears, and walking through every labyrinth I could find. It took me two years to discern God's call on my life because I wanted to make sure God was truly calling me—and I wanted to understand the call.

I felt heavily burdened, but I didn't know why.

7. What occurred that enabled you to overcome the resistance to answering the call?

In 2009, an Episcopal priest explained that I was not responsible for saving anyone because Christ had already done that. When I heard that, the burden was immediately lifted off me. I was then able to move forward in my call. I continued to be in prayer and meditation as I heard and followed God's call.

8. What was the time frame between receiving the call and saying yes with appropriate action?

Two years.

9. What role did the church play in answering or not answering the call immediately?

I was fifty-four when I discussed my call with my district superintendent. I was encouraged to participate in the Course of Study, which takes six years. In addition, I felt like I needed to know about the United Methodist denomination before I set foot in a United Methodist Church pulpit.

10. *Were there any spiritual disciplines that played a role in your resistance or acceptance of the call? Tell the stories.*

Prayer, fasting, meditation, and labyrinths have played critical roles in my discernment process and enabled me to accept the call to ordained ministry.

11. *In retrospect, how do you see God's hand at work in your life that prepared you for ordained ministry?*

At age fifty-six, I began seminary at Candler School of Theology at Emory University because I was very impressed with the care given my son during his three weeks of Youth Theological Institute (YTI) at Candler. My pastor also attended Candler in the summers, and I saw how enthusiastic she was upon her return. She brought that excitement to the parishioners in the congregation. Candler School of Theology appeared to be perfect in helping develop my spiritual gifts and affirming my call.

Upon the completion of my studies at Candler School of Theology, I returned to the Mississippi Conference and utilized the experiences afforded me. I planned to use the creative techniques in ministry to touch people in my path. The passion of being a servant leader has been used to enrich the lives of the faith community. In retrospect, my twenty-nine years of teaching played a vital role in my effectiveness as a pastor.

The experience of working with adults and children has been invaluable as I pastor people of all ages. The importance of communicating and encouraging children to grow and do their best is very much like communicating and encouraging the parishioners to grow in their faith. Knowing how children are at different levels and growing at different speeds, through God's grace, I can see the same in the people I serve. I was passionate as a teacher, and I have a greater passion as a pastor. I can see how God is using my experience as a teacher to make me a greater and better pastor for His kingdom.

12. *When you accepted the call to ministry, what was the response from persons in your life?*

I have been very blessed to have nothing but positive responses from my announcement of my call. My children have been very supportive. My eldest son is a Baptist pastor, and his support is encouraging. My husband is an Episcopal deacon and supports my call. My siblings have called on me as a resource to respond to their questions about faith. The support from everyone has been reassuring, and it demonstrates how they also see the call God has poured into my life.

PHASE 2

1. *Tell the story of your first three years while meeting the requirements necessary for elder's or deacon's ordination or for local pastor's requirements. What were some of your struggles and victories as you pursued answering the call?*

- *Share your stories with the Board(s) of Ordained Ministry. In what ways were they helpful? Did you have any identifiable issues that you were told to improve upon?*
- *If you were assigned to a church(s) during those first three years, what relationships did you have with the parishioners and the community?*
- *When you attended seminary or licensing school, what were your experiences with faculty, staff, and peers? Include the specific years?*

I met with a mentor for a year prior to going to the superintendent or to my church to verify the call. I went before the district committee on ministry (DCOM) as a certified local pastor. I didn't want to pastor, but I went to seminary to know more about the UMC, its processes, and its procedures. I had taught school for twenty-nine years, and some of the skills needed for teaching were also needed for ministry such as compassion, patience, embracing differences, and being intentional with diversity. However, I needed to learn more about baptism, the Wesley Quadrilateral, and other things.

I had a struggle with the fact that I was fifty-four years old, which was older than most people pursuing elder's orders. The district superintendent (DS) was more inclined for me to pursue the "Course of Study" because of my age. I was led to pursue ordination as an ordained elder. God calls whom he will, and He knows their ages. God calls—not the UMC or its processes.

When I finished seminary, I was assigned to these two churches for five years. Some members of the congregations knew me from past experiences, including the chancellor of Emory University. One congregation was a very academic congregation. The young people were very helpful. The PPR and trustees at the church were also helpful.

When I went before the Board of Ordained Ministry (BOOM), I didn't answer the question on the Wesley Quadrilateral very well. At the end of the meeting, they asked me what the committee could do for me, and I asked the committee to pray for me. The second time I went before BOOM, I was asked a theological question, and I did not answer the question very well. I stopped, took a deep breath, and prayed within until I got peace. I then proceeded, and I did not have any difficulty with BOOM. There were no issues identified in the second interview.

2. *Share your stories of each individual appointment since beginning the process for ordination until 2016. Include the following:*

- *What lessons did you learn from each appointment?*
- *What meaningful relationships were established? Include personal, professional, and church member relationships.*
- *What was your personal and church financial state?*
- *Relate any successes or challenges you faced in each appointment. Were there any personal events that affected your ministry (weddings, deaths, or illnesses?)*

- *Relate any successes or challenges you faced in each appointment. Were there any personal events that affected your ministry (weddings, deaths, illnesses, etc.)?*
- *What Methodist, national, local, or world events affected your appointments? Explain how.*
- *Have any of the meaningful relationships established with your parishioners been continued over the years?*

FIRST APPOINTMENT:

PASTOR OF ST. PAUL UMC AND MT. ZION UM CHURCHES

I learned to listen better to God and to the members. I learned to trust God more for God will do His part. God is working in me and the church at the same time. I learned to pray more, and I experienced God's revelation through prayer. For instance, the church didn't have a choir for one year, but God revealed to me to leave it alone. I left it alone. After one year, the choir came back, and I could see God working on my patience. Some people left because I was female, but I served them if they needed me for visitations or other services. Serving them enabled me to practice the Christian ethic of doing good to others who have not been good to me.

Meaningful relationships began to develop, and love increased. I suggested we work around the church property, and as we worked, we prayed, praised, and anointed each person's house. Members have learned to love, trust, listen to, and open up to me as pastor. Our lives are more closely in tune, and there is definitely more trust.

The church financial state at one church was okay, and they had savings. The other church has a mortgage, but they are looking to pay it off early.

My personal finances were not good. I had no income while in seminary except my husband's income. When I began pastoring, my income from the two churches was low. I am now receiving a pension from teaching, which is helping to pay off my student loans.

One of the most noticeable successes during my tenure is a growth in the closeness of the congregation in caring for each other and for the community.

I have established some meaningful relationships during my pastorate, but since I have not been moved to another church, it remains to be seen if those same relationships will be continued. On the other hand, there are other meaningful relationships in the church that will remain firm because we were friends before I started to pastor the churches.

3. Do you see any of your life stories depicted in the lives of the saints in the Bible? Was it helpful to see yourself in scripture as you journeyed in your appointment?

Presently, God is training me to understand Paul. I see God working in my spirit to be at peace until God calls me home or to another church. While I remain, I am to glorify God in everything I do and say. It is a blessing to share that I am at peace with my son who is not attending any church. I said, "If I leave, God has my back, and you will know it is OK, but I am concerned about your soul."

Like Paul, God is helping me understand more of who He is and to praise Him even in my faults. I am to trust God completely. I can see God transforming me to be, act, think, and see like Paul. I am learning how to see and hear in more loving ways than ever before. I have a vision as I see God's love pouring through others—and the entire creation.

4. If you were the first Black woman, or among the firsts, in any of your appointments, state those firsts, and tell the stories. What words of wisdom would you pass on to others who may become pioneers during their ministry?

I am the first Black woman assigned to the two churches I serve.

What words of wisdom would you pass on to others who may become pioneers during their ministry?

The words of wisdom I would pass on to others who may become pioneers during their ministry are many.

- They should love the people God has placed them to serve.
- Don't take every situation personally.
- Those persons who can't see God in your being appointed at their church will leave but pray for them anyway.
- Pray for those who remain that they will be able to hear from God as well.
- Pray for God to love your congregation and give you a spirit of love as Christ loved the church.
- Pray for yourself to respond to your congregation with compassion, regardless of how hard it may be.
- Pray for God to keep you from acting out of a spirit of anger.
- Do what God has called you to do and be what God has called you to be.
- When it gets too hard, call another Black clergywoman or a pastor you trust to give you godly counsel, so you can vent and share the journey.
- Develop prayer partnerships with other Black clergywomen so you can pray for one another ongoing.

5. *In hindsight, how could the annual conference and/or other UM personnel be more helpful when signing Black clergywomen as firsts in a given area of ministry?*

- The annual conference could be more intentional in preparing the church and the pastor for cross-racial appointments. For instance, they could have the Black clergywoman to preach or teach for special programs and/or worship, providing the atmosphere for the Black clergywoman to be embraced and not eaten up by wolves. Preaching would allow God to work more.
- She should not be suddenly "thrown in" on the congregation. There should be opportunities to interact and relate in

some ways at least six months in advance. There should be intentionality in avoiding the shock treatment because it is equally shocking for the Black clergywoman and the church where she is appointed.

6. *What personal gifts and graces have been assets to you during your years of ministry? Be specific and relate how they have been helpful.*

- I have a passion for learning for myself and others.
- God's love is amazing even to me, and God has built on that. I love more, and I share what is working for me, freely, with the congregation.
- I learned the principles of behavior modification in school, and I loved teaching them to the students. I apply those same concepts as I minister to my congregations.
- God gives me the gift of discernment in the jail ministry. When I am interacting with the jail personnel, I can tell them when they are not okay.

They ask, "How do you know?" I say, "God gives me the ability to know." I tell them that I will be praying for them. People know and sense they are valued and cared for as I assure them that we are all children of God. I glorify God in all the gifts he has given to me. I know and express that it is not about me; it is about God. I share my gifts with members of the church and with others in life. God is helping me become a better pastor, a better person, and a better Christian.

7. *List any particular accomplishments or honors conferred during your years of ministry.*

- I am honored to serve on the Residency in Ministry Board. It is a board that processes candidates from the time of commissioning until they are ordained. It is a three-year process: First year—get acquainted; Second year—small groups; Third year—ordained elder process and questioning.

- I serve as mentor for those discerning their call.
- I am an instructor for lay servants in prayer, worship, and workshops.
- By the power of the Holy Spirit, I teach Bible study to thirty men through our jail ministry. This ministry has been ongoing for eight years and counting.

CONCLUSION

Black clergywomen became pastors because their primary call to ordained ministry came after intense prayer times and being certain they were answering yes to the call from Jesus Christ. Their commitment to Jesus Christ was the guiding force that gave them strength to persevere, in love and forgiveness, under all circumstances they faced along the journey. Having intense prayer lives is a hallmark for Black clergywomen. In addition, many are prayer warriors who have committed themselves to extended days of prayer and fasting.

Observing the history of Black clergywomen, we can see that it was the movement of the Holy Spirit that empowered these clergywomen to foster spiritual, financial, and numerical growth in the churches and institutions under their pastoral leadership despite opposition, resistance, and injustice.

Black clergywomen have accepted the call to ordained ministry for decades in the United Methodist Church. In doing so, they inherited the struggle against racism, sexism, ageism, economic discrimination, and other "isms" in the church. Frequently, they were placed in small-membership churches, sometimes in rural or small-town isolated areas where few or no Blacks lived, and/or in churches where the salary was minimum by denominational standards. In most cases, no preparatory work was conducted to address the racism and sexism that were preexistent when the Black clergywomen were placed in cross-racial appointments in White churches.

Most Black clergywomen in cross-racial appointments were pioneers with little or no local church, district, conference, or peer support, having to navigate their pathways in isolation without advocacy. Often, they could only trust and depend on Jesus, who called them. When Jesus was all they had, they discovered in profound ways that Jesus was all they needed. It bears noting that some clergywomen were also active in desegregation of schools, civil rights events, and other social justice activities.

Some of the experiences of racism, sexism, ageism, and economic discrimination that were shared, but not recorded in the stories due to privacy protection, include:

- Verbal abuse.
- False accusations.
- Physical attacks.
- Moving the Black clergywoman when conflict arises rather than working to resolve the conflict.
- Senior pastors who need racism and sexism training.
- Micromanaging the gifts of the Black clergywomen.
- Marginalizing and shutting out Black clergywomen when racism and sexism occur.
- Denial of any racism or sexism on the part of the congregations or institutions, but blaming and punishing the Black clergywomen.
- Sexual harassment.
- Rare appointments to high-paying churches.
- Reducing the salary when Black clergywomen are appointed.
- Lack of denominational help and support when congregations are antagonistic. toward the Black clergywomen and engaging in conflictual behavior.

The power of the Holy Spirit was evident, despite the "isms," in touching the hearts of church members, judicatory leaders, colleagues, and members of the community. Some took action to assist in correcting the ills of racism, sexism, ageism, and economic discrimination on a case-by-case basis.

Black clergywomen persevered to become pastors. With approximately seven hundred Black clergywomen in the UMC, a small number were appointed and hired in positions at national church levels, in seminaries and universities, as conference staff, and as district superintendents while a precious few were elected as bishops.

These stories provide a written historical legacy of Black clergywomen telling their own stories while making history in the church.

Since the global protests following the death of George Floyd, the United Methodist Church has intensified its commitment to dismantle racism, but questions still remain: "How will the specific dismantling of racism, sexism, ageism, and economic discrimination against Black clergywomen be addressed?"

Black clergywomen continue to be pioneers in the United Methodist Church of America. Their stories can be valuable resources for denominational leaders as we work together to dismantle "isms" and become the embodiment of Christ-love to all people.

The end poem *Patches of Praise* describes the collective responses of Black clergywomen to their journeys.

PATCHES OF PRAISE

I pondered in my heart the events of my life
That weaved in and out
Like the strands
Of a beautifully patched quilt.
There were many brilliant colors and hues
Many textures, and a variety of fabrics.

The intricate strands symbolized the simple
Yet, complex order of my life
Which existed even in the midst of chaos.
I praised the Lord!

The colors and hues reminded me
That my life has been touched
By the same artistic hand that painted
The rainbow in the magnificent sky.
I praised the Lord!

Some textures were rough.
I remembered those hard places in life
That required perseverance and tenacity.
I praised the Lord!

Some textures were smooth.
I reflected on those moments
Of ease and tranquility
I praised the Lord!

There was delicate silk.
I saw the times when
I was fragile and needed tender love and care.
I praised the Lord!

The wool sent my mind soaring
As I recalled, I am a sheep
I am dumb
Before the shearer
I praised the Lord!

Ah, the cotton so soft and puffy
Would not let me forget
That a strong wind would blow me away
Unless I remained anchored to the Vine
I praised the Lord!

The many patches touched my heart deeply
I was intimately reminded of the times
When the harshness and brutality of life
Broke me and tore me in many pieces
Yet, the loving Savior
Stooped down, gave me a drink,
Oiled my wounds
And nursed me back to health and wholeness.

Tell me, wise one,
How can I open my lips except
To praise the Lord?

—Josephine Whitely-Fields, 1989

Printed in the United States
By Bookmasters